LEADER REACH

Essays On the Dynamics of Values,

Communication, Spirituality, and Power

In Leadership

LEADER REACH

Essays On the Dynamics of Values,

Communication, Spirituality, and Power

In Leadership

BONNY V. BANKS

STEWARD PUBLISHING

LEADER REACH: Essays On the Dynamics of Values:
Communication, Spirituality, and Power In Leadership
Revised edition
Steward Publishing, Union, New Jersey

Copyright 2009, 2013 by Bonny V. Banks

Requests for permission to use or reproduce material from this book should be directed to:
Permissions@StewardPublishing.com

Library of Congress Cataloguing-in-Publication Data

Banks, Bonny V.
Leader Reach: Essays On the Dynamics of Values,
Communication, Spirituality, and Power In Leadership/
Bonny V. Banks
Includes bibliographical references
ISBN 978-0-9796106-1-5
ISBN 0-9796106-1-3

Printed in the United States of America

The paper used in this publication meets the requirements of the American National Standard for Permanence of Paper for Publication and Documents in Libraries and Archives 239.48-1992

To Daddy,
a wise leader

CONTENTS

Acknowledgements

Special thanks to you, Father,
for Your love, guidance, and inspiration.
Thanks to my family for your invaluable support,
inspiration, encouragement, and especially for the
late nights, Penelope.

INTRODUCTION:

LEADERSHIP AND VALUES

Typically, organizations and leaders espouse a set of values and convey the same to workers and customers alike. Although leaders verbalize and present a set of values on company vision statements, mission statements, web pages, and letterheads, *true* core values will always display in leaders' actions, behaviors, decisions, policies, and pursuits. Values are birthed out of a set of beliefs that individuals and organizations (through leaders) develop about themselves, their place in the world, relationships, the environment, morality, and spirituality. Values have neither the obligation nor inclination toward being good or bad. Values simply represent truth, and if there is one virtue to be sought after, it is consistency between asserted and demonstrated values.

The dynamics of communication, spirituality, and power in leader/follower relationships often reveal contradictions in values execution. Much of the perplexity followers and observers experience in attempting to reconcile leaders' actions has to do with disparities between stated and perceptible values. How a leader says one thing and does another, so to speak, leaves observers wondering what confidence, if any, should be placed in the leader's words. In order to quell the confusion brought on by inconsistencies, followers consciously and unconsciously make independent determinations about leaders and organizations' *true* values based upon apparent behaviors.

Organizations suffer when followers have little confidence in leader assurances. Where there is distrust, individuals and groups determine to bide their time and prioritize self or group interests over those of the organization. This is a form of quiet rebellion, more affably characterized as an autonomous type of follower self-empowerment.

One way to avoid the anarchistic thinking that can easily begin to simmer beneath the surface of daily operations is to invest in formalized follower empowerment initiatives that encourage participation on all levels. In so doing, leaders develop an avenue through which organizations align stated values with actionable results. Leaders who actualize trust through decentralized structuring, inclusion, tacit knowledge sharing, and risk taking, for instance, learn to circumvent barriers to cohesiveness and flow. Trust, as a demonstrated value, ultimately stimulates the creativity often suppressed by insecurity and the aversion to risk. A values based approach encourages partnership between leaders and followers as they work together toward mutually agreed upon goals and objectives.

This is not to suggest that follower empowerment requires a structure of democratization, but rather involvement that workers consider meaningful. To simply solicit workers' opinions on choosing a printer for the newly devised goals and implementation schedule, for example, excludes followers from meaningful involvement in the project as a whole. Workers would much rather contribute to process and development rather than be relegated to deciding upon inconsequential particulars in the end. Developing and infusing collaboration initiatives can cultivate trust and respect for the contributions of both leaders and followers throughout the organization.

Empowerment, both for leaders and followers, is perceived and defined out of values. Authentic participative leadership allows leaders to gain followers' confidence and establish relationship based on mutual vulnerability. Leader transparency endeavors to diminish the perception of the invincible, autocratic superior, and aptly so as contemporary followers are becoming increasingly unresponsive to despotic, non-inclusive style leadership - and do not mind saying so.

Because autocratic authority works against the benefits of collaborative leadership, what I discover, more often than not, is the disarming effect that the participative approach has on followers as leaders determine to meet followers at eye level. Workers appear to feel empowered by the realization that their contributions are not only sought after, but also actualized through genuine shared leadership initiatives. Traditional leaders in the contemporary workforce have to reconcile conventional wisdom with the changing landscape of structuring based on fluidity, inclusion, and environmental sensitivity. Because client based planning has to begin within the walls of the organization, leaders must deliberately create opportunities for follower input and meaningful participation. Leaders who place high value on follower input may consider a participative or situational leadership agenda.

Participative leadership, also referred to as collaborative leadership, joint leadership, and shared leadership, is categorized as a type of values based behavioral model where leadership style is characterized by the actions of the leader to involve workers in meaningful decision-making and goal setting. Participative leadership, in its truest sense, endeavors to empower followers and cultivate trust in the leader/follower relationship. Situational leadership takes into account conditional circumstances that determine a leader's involvement as measured by the follower's competency and commitment to specific tasks. Leaders can learn to employ a situational approach without necessarily formalizing the process. It is a way of treating followers as individuals and adapting a style of leadership that adequately corresponds to a worker's specific needs and abilities. In short, situational leadership emphasizes the individuality of followers and discourages a broad spectrum approach to leader-follower interactions.

Situational leadership is similar to participative leadership in that both are follower oriented and seek to empower followers as a goal. The difference lies is in the assumptions of participative leadership. In participative leadership theory, involvement and interest on the part of followers are assumed. Low interest is considered interest nonetheless and the expectation is that with enough empowering actions on the part of the leader, follower interest will manifest. There are times, however, when leaders may discover that followers resist participative ideas and any empowerment agenda initiated by leadership. This resistance usually translates to a lack of interest or trust toward leaders or the organization. While followers may not arbitrarily shy away from the notion of empowerment per se, reluctance is often rooted in the perception of values ambiguity within the organization.

Typically, participative leadership implementation strategies involve varying levels of employee involvement in decision-making. Theorist, Gary Yukl, describes four distinct methods that leaders draw upon for decision-making: (a) autocratic decisions, (b) consultation, (c) joint decisions, and (d) delegation. [1] Autocratic decision-making is top-down leadership with no collaboration or input on the part of subordinates. Consultation seeks to involve employees to the extent that a leader may select and present an issue for discussion in an effort to solicit follower input and suggestions. Albeit with the consultation approach, the leader retains the power to make final decisions after careful consideration of followers' input. Yukl makes a distinction between consultation and joint decision-making. Joint decision-making puts the leader at equal footing with followers. That is, the leader reserves no rank in the decision. The agreement from the onset is that the leader will participate as a group member and contribute to consensus building without evoking any undue pressure or influence due to the leader's authority. Delegation assigns responsibility away from the leader.

Early in my career in education administration, I developed advisory committees that consisted of members of stakeholder groups including students, parents, teachers, staff, and community members. Within these committees, I employed joint decision-making as my approach to shared leadership. At a typical meeting we brought ideas to a discussion and made decisions together without my input or opinions as the leader carrying greater weight. The groups' memberships grew appreciatively as participants experienced meaningful collaboration and having their decisions upheld whether I agreed with specific suggestions or not. In so doing, one effort toward authentic collaboration helped to cultivate an overall environment of inclusion, empowerment, and trust.

While shared leadership has its benefits, not all situations or environments are conducive for its implementation. In highly bureaucratic, centralized organizations where little opportunity for autonomy exists, leaders are more like managers who merely oversee and facilitate daily operations. Unlike leaders working in creative environments, these leader/managers are not able to dedicate the bulk of their efforts to concentrating on strategic planning, innovation, or new ideas. Instead, they are saddled with regulations, processes, procedures, and policies that leave little to no room for visioning or creative musing. As well, efforts toward collaboration are often treated with suspicion in settings where top-down, dictatorial leadership has traditionally been the norm. It is also not unusual to discover that organizational and worker values differ in centralized, autocratic environments. When there is an appreciative difference in values, leaders may opt to employ a situational approach to leadership.

When I moved from a highly successful school district where there was consistency between organizational values, leader values, and staff values to a district where this was not the case, my leadership approach had to change to fit the current environment. It was through this experience that I encountered the limitations of participative leadership. My new district was a low performing maze of strife and political infighting where apathy, low expectations, and indifference toward students defined the status quo. Although I enjoyed less autonomy in this new district, I hoped to share what little authority I had in an effort to raise morale among a fiercely embittered staff. My collaborative approach to goal setting and decision-making did not work and had little appeal. Many of the staff who participated on the surface took our roundtable discussions as opportunities to angrily vent and oppose each other. Bargaining unit representatives were everywhere asserting the rights of their members to limit interactions with administrators, students, and parents. My values and those of the district and its top leaders, including many with whom I worked, were in dire conflict.

Here was a situation in which the organization's asserted values and observable values conflicted. The district had touted itself publicly and on paper as a safe haven of excellence for children where dedication and commitment to quality education were its highest values. Yet, the district communicated its *actual* values every time its top leaders made decisions that contradicted their collective calling to put students' needs first. One example included a decision to acquiesce to a labor union that forbade teachers to tutor students (for pay) for as few as thirty minutes after school one day per week. In practice, this school district demonstrated more value for political camaraderie than it did for its *stated* values of dedication and commitment to students.

The very organization that pledged to safeguard their main stakeholders' (students) interests by cultivating a supportive and caring learning environment worked, in effect, to impede the same. Disparate objectives and constant strivings against students' interests revealed the contradiction between the district's stated and manifest values. When organizations and leaders assert one set of values and demonstrate another, the former appears disingenuous at best. Because of the conflicting value systems in this new school district, I had to employ a situational approach to leadership before any participative agenda could find acceptance. It became my endeavor to search out staff members with whom I shared common values and find some way to cultivate each individual's skills and potential one by one.

Researchers, Hersey and Blanchard, developed a situational grid that illustrates follower directed leadership. Hersey and Blanchard term their four approaches, directing, coaching, participating, and delegating. [2] For a follower who has a low level of competence or understanding about a particular job function, and who may not necessarily exhibit interest or commitment toward the assignment, the leader may need to provide individualized instruction, close supervision, and regular positive feedback. Alternatively, for an employee who has a high level of competence and commitment toward the job, the leader is able to delegate more responsibility and allow the employee to work independently. Between these two extremes are examples of employees who exhibit alternating levels of competence and commitment.

In the case of a worker with high competence but low interest or confidence, the leader may need to help the follower discover empowerment in the task through formalized coaching. If an employee is lacking in the skills to perform a task, yet is enthusiastic and committed to seeing it through, the leader only has to provide specific and well-defined instruction. There is no need, in the latter instance, for the leader to attempt to motivate the follower. The follower simply needs the leader to participate until the follower is comfortable in undertaking the task with minimal assistance or supervision. This follower is then able work independently.

Situational leadership is designed to assist followers in evolving and developing from a level of dependence to levels of independence and interdependence. The leader works with followers along the grid to navigate followers' professional growth. The overall endeavor of the situational approach is to challenge followers to evolve toward their highest professional and personal development. Continuous personal development leads to the self-actualization that most people aspire to. There are many approaches to leading others, and whether a leader chooses to be autocratic, collaborative, or a coach, follower outcomes will always affect the organization.

Unlike one school of thought which suggests that leading is all about followers, I suggest that leadership is about everyone, leaders as well as followers. Leaders who understand follower empowerment stand to earn followers' respect, trust, and loyalty. At the same time, empowered, spiritually fulfilled leaders bring valuable aspects of spiritual formation to the follower developmental process. Spiritually attuned leaders take responsibility for cultivating leadership in followers by helping followers realize their individual potential. This is a tall order and not necessarily a part of every leader's written job description. Nevertheless, conscientious leaders have to concede that organizations benefit by leaders taking interest in employees' personal as well as professional development.

The role and function of workers have historically been associated with task management and perfunctory responsibilities. However, since the revelations of the early Hawthorne Experiments, when Elton Mayo hypothesized about the possibility of artificially controlling and predicting worker performance, consideration for worker needs has surfaced as an undeniable component upon which organizational outcomes depend. For over a hundred years workers have been trying to get the point across to company leaders that organizations that treat their employees as mere physical beings ignore the best of what workers have to offer, and by so doing, perform beneath their capacities. Progressive leaders understand that today's followers want and need to feel empowered in their organizational environments. While economic incentives are crucial, monetary reward does not provide the exclusive motivation for employee production and satisfaction. It is the integration of values centered leadership that ushers in the meaningfulness workers seek.

The chapters that follow highlight three dynamics that define values more than any other aspects of the leader/follower relationship. They are communication, spirituality, and power.

Communication is essential for understanding expectations, building perceptions, and imparting beliefs. Leaders communicate with followers through their words, actions, decisions, and behaviors. For effective leader/follower communication, both must ensure that messages are unambiguous and convey comprehensible values to others. Leaders consciously and unconsciously express values and perceptions in all of their interactions with followers. It is also important to recognize how perceptions, especially across cultures, manifest in communication strategies. Organizations and leaders who value diversity, for example, will invest in cultural competence and sensitivity. The weight of a leader's actions informs the truth of a leader's words. In the same way, organizational mantras are measured against observable policies and pursuits.

Spirituality comprises the values and beliefs of individuals. Set apart from religion or New Age ideology, spirituality has to do with a person's well-being and ability to express values related to general fulfillment.

Organizational leaders have to begin to manifestly express understanding of the importance of spirituality and spiritual fulfillment as both inform worker satisfaction. From the onset of the Industrial Revolution through the late fifties and early sixties, workers observed the practice of leaving personal needs and problems at home when they went to work. The gradual but steady evolution of the assertive worker has, over succeeding decades, produced a generation that has become the polar opposite of its early predecessors.

Unlike many traditional workers who remained with employers for decades, the newest entrants to the workforce are likely to follow the trend set by younger baby boomers of changing employers 11 times before they reach age 42.[3] In today's work culture, especially with the infusing of technology that imposes upon workers to remain almost constantly engaged with the job, the lines of separation between work and home are becoming increasingly imprecise. This is part of the reason the twenty-first century worker no longer views work as an end unto itself, but as an element of a broader and intensely personal reality. Workers today inform their spirituality by a well-defined set of personal values and beliefs working in tandem to shape and influence every aspect of life and truth.

Related to spirituality is the issue of power. The equitable acquisition and distribution of power are arguably among the chief determinants of desirable leader-follower interactions. Power is the ability of one individual to affect the behaviors, actions, and decisions of another. In many workplace environments the treatment of power is the distinguishing factor between workers whose values, beliefs, and needs are deliberately considered and those whose needs are ignored. To qualify this statement, I am suggesting that empowerment in a vacuum could be accomplished with a simple role change from follower to leader or from worker to entrepreneur. Empowerment in the organizational context, however, is more about the facility and freedom to express certain spiritual and emotional needs in the workplace while having those needs not be alien to or in conflict with organizational values. Irrespective of what a leader verbalizes, values inform truth by what a leader does.

Throughout the pages of this book, the reader will discover ways in which leaders and organizations display and convey their *true* values and how those values surface in communication, spirituality, and power. By *true*, I mean actual, authentic, unrehearsed, and unscripted. Inspiring words take real meaning when corresponding actions give credence to them. In the case of values conflict and inconsistency, the voice of action first exposes then delegitimizes and finally repudiates mere rhetoric.

13

THE DYNAMIC OF

COMMUNICATION

"GO AHEAD. I'M LISTENING..."

Have you ever had an occasion to walk into your supervisor's office for a scheduled meeting, to ask a quick question, or share a heartfelt concern only to sit and watch your supervisor text, type, open mail, or read memos while you spoke? What about the time you thought your supervisor was taking copious notes to capture all your great ideas? She had interrupted you mid-sentence to call in her secretary to retrieve what you later learned was your supervisor's list of excursions for her family's vacation cruise itinerary. How did you feel when you discovered that your supervisor's entire note taking had absolutely nothing to do with you or the nature of your concerns?

After the secretary left the office, you remained quiet until invited to begin speaking again. The telephone rang. Your supervisor answered the phone, talked for about a minute, ended the call, and placed another "quick call." You whispered an apology and rose to leave. Your supervisor, while holding the phone in one hand and covering its speaker with the other, gestured for you to remain as she whispered, "Go ahead. I'm listening."

Or, how about the time you were sitting engrossed at your desk feeling overwhelmed and inundated with work and deadlines. You were checking emails when one of your team members approached the threshold of your office and asked apologetically, "Hey, got a minute?" After pushing from your mind regretful thoughts about instituting an open door policy, you looked up from your keyboard, smiled, and invited your colleague in. Had you noticed that your hand remained fastened to your mouse?

Communication is about messages - messages sent and messages received. How often has it been said, "It's not what you say, but how you say it?" Instinctively, one supposes that tone of voice and word choice matter the most in communicating information to others. However, listening is just as important. As a hospice volunteer, I learned in my training that a very viable difference exists between passive listening and *active* listening.

Active listening is a skill one must practice and improve over time. Active listening is when one deliberately chooses to engage the speaker through eye contact, nodding, and other physical validations like positioning oneself toward rather than away from the speaker. Active listeners dedicate the mental energy to process what the speaker is saying and resist the temptation to formulate responses prematurely.

Have you ever attempted to express a heartfelt concern with someone only to notice the person just waiting for you to take a breath so she could chime right in? How does it make you feel when your supervisor denies you eye contact or when coworkers exhibit blank stares during your presentations? Consider Brenda Fields.*

---

* Name changed to a fictitious name

Brenda Fields is the president and CEO of her own investment firm. Brenda and her team of eight manage nearly 200 individual and commercial accounts while pursuing new clients daily. Brenda normally spends 12-13 hours at the office before going home to work for an additional three to four hours nightly. Aside from working most weekends, Brenda works on holidays and has not taken a vacation with her family in the seven years since leaving her job as an investment banker. Brenda prides herself on having superior people skills and enjoys a reputation of being there when her clients need her. Clients know they can contact Brenda any time day or night via phone, fax, or email and expect a quick and timely response. Most of Brenda's referrals have come from her reputation for being accessible, informed, and collaborative.

What Brenda does not know is that she has also earned the distinction by her staff of "Blackberry Queen." Brenda's teenage children refer to her behind her back, as "Virtual Mom." After throwing Brenda's mobile phone out of their bedroom window during an intense argument, Brenda's husband left their home for the second time in four years. He had often complained that he "wanted a wife not an appointment!"

Brenda had always enjoyed a demanding career and was no stranger to taking work home. Her family could, in the past, count on spending quality time with Brenda on most weekends and holidays. Brenda and her family used to take regular vacations twice a year and enjoyed local outings as well. Since launching her business, though,

Brenda has been working incessantly. Brenda's family had pledged their support and Brenda had promised to ensure quality time at home and away from the office. Initially, Brenda would work as long as she needed to at the office yet be completely available to her family once she arrived home. Twice during the first month, Brenda brought "an hour's worth of work" home. Within three months, Brenda was conducting phone conferences at home and pouring over paperwork nightly.

At the office, Brenda's staff could count on Brenda's physical presence in the office. Yet somehow the team learned to reconcile Brenda's unavailability to staff by citing the tremendous responsibility Brenda shoulders in running such a fast-paced and demanding business.

One Friday afternoon there was something of an explosion of anger in the vestibule of the office. Three of Brenda's team members and two support staff were yelling and accusing each other of impeding deadlines and sabotaging others' efforts with clients. Brenda had been on a conference call when the sheer volume of noise literally drew her out of her office to investigate. Blackberry in hand, Brenda approached the scene and after muting her call, sternly scolded everyone for a "despicable display of unprofessionalism!"

As individuals began explaining what was going on, Brenda interrupted stating that she had a call to finish. Brenda admonished the staff to immediately return to their desks and email her their concerns. She would set up a meeting with everyone later. With that, Brenda turned and walked back to her office shutting the door behind her to resume her conference call. Brenda never noticed one exasperated staff member who had been hovering over a chair right behind her. As the crowd stood processing Brenda's response, one person quit on the spot and stormed out of the building. Another burst into tears. The person who had been hovering over the chair began hyperventilating and had to be taken by ambulance to the local hospital emergency room where he was later released and sent home to rest for two weeks.

Although Brenda later scheduled a meeting with staff to discuss the vestibule incident, the meeting never took place. Three times since the original scheduled date the meeting was postponed; twice because Brenda needed to participate in conference calls with existing clients and once to consummate a contract with a new client.

When I arrived at this plush and professional suite of offices, I noticed that for all the warmth of the décor, the atmosphere had a distinct coldness. People smiled and greeted each other in a perfunctory manner. It was reminiscent of watching mindless thinking in motion. I also observed Brenda and her interactions with the staff. Brenda carried her Blackberry with her at all times and was almost constantly engaged in its functions. Whether texting, talking, or emailing, Brenda seemed to always be on the phone. One staff member I interviewed jokingly described Brenda's Blackberry as being a literal extension of her arm.

I learned that most of Brenda's emailing was to staff who worked right alongside her in the office. For whatever reason, Brenda appeared to prefer electronic communication rather than person-to-person contact. Brenda sent incessant text messages to her husband and children and received constant calls from clients. I sat as a silent observer during Brenda's fiscal meetings with staff and noticed that Brenda hardly ever looked away from her computer the whole time someone spoke with her. Brenda hardly even paid attention to team members' presentations.

Brenda's staff would typically begin impromptu meetings with Brenda by apologizing and offering assurances of brevity. Because Brenda insisted on being kept abreast of the minutest detail, her staff had to confer with her for direction at every juncture in managing individual accounts. Staff members attempted to establish a connection with Brenda but to no avail. While staff spoke and asked questions, Brenda would read, text, answer, and initiate emails. Once every minute or two, Brenda would look up over her glasses and back to her keyboard. If a staff member paused mid-sentence to check Brenda's engagement level, Brenda would say, right on cue and without looking up, "Go ahead. I'm listening."

One thing Brenda does not realize is that no matter inviting her words may be, her actions send a totally different message and people are internalizing the latter. What Brenda considers multitasking, others consider self-indulgent, diminishing, and rude. Brenda's decision to continually check and send emails during meetings with staff communicates distraction, disinterest, and inaccessibility. Brenda's practice of hardly looking up from her keyboard while staff members attempt to converse with her sends a message, however unintentional, that the staff's concerns are not worth Brenda's time or full attention. When Brenda answers telephone calls or sends text messages during interactions with her employees, Brenda communicates indifference to individuals' needs to be heard and validated. Brenda's 12-14 hour days spent at the office and late nights dedicated to working from home communicate clear messages of unavailability to her family.

Whether or not Brenda intends her actions to be alienating to others matters little. Perception is what creates reality for Brenda's colleagues and family. Life is a series of choices and Brenda, when faced with staff, clients, and family each vying for her time and attention, makes decisions based on Brenda's *true* values. Irrespective of what Brenda verbalizes to her employees or family members in moments of sentimental appreciation, Brenda consistently communicates her authenticity and her truth with every decision she makes regarding her time, resources, and attention. Brenda decides to engage in what makes Brenda feel the most empowered, accomplished, and productive.

Brenda's paradox is that Brenda believes she is genuine and sincere when she expresses her love to those whose support she depends upon daily, but Brenda's constant inward focus diminishes her ability to perceive the needs of others or her own narcissism and the atrophy it is creating in her business and relationships.

Not all is lost, however. Brenda always glances over to say, "Go ahead. I'm listening..."

LEADER COMMUNICATION AND FOLLOWER PRODUCTIVITY

Organizational performance depends upon several factors including follower productivity. While not the only indicator of organizational success, worker productivity ranks among the paramount influences. In projecting productivity, leaders typically utilize a quantitative formula that takes into account several variances, one of which is internal conditions. At times, followers fall short of leader expectations without any obvious cause. While it is quite simple to hold followers responsible for disparities between leader expectations and follower output, one particular factor begs early consideration. Aside from matters like group homogeneity and scheduling, one area often overlooked is the affect leader communication has on worker productivity. The manner in which leaders communicate with followers affects follower interpretation, motivation, and eventual output. By observing leader communication habits and practices, leaders can gain valuable insight into ways to sharpen the skill of communicating with followers, thus improving follower productivity and organizational performance as a whole.

First, consistency in behaviors and expectations among leaders communicates order, stability, and synchronization. Followers, in order to produce unreservedly, need to feel safe and part of a well-functioning and cohesive team. Leaders operating in various capacities within an organization display highly individualized approaches to the leader/follower relationship; and followers who answer to more than one member of a leadership team face the challenge of adjusting to diverse temperaments and leadership styles. This can be especially difficult for followers, especially when one leader minimizes work and communication standards upheld by another. When leaders are not all on the same page, followers are left out of the loop completely. The goal in creating the predictability characteristic of a safe environment is not the absence of personality or color. Rather, it is the development and appreciation of uniformity in expectations that ensures followers of the absence of chaos, which so easily hinders performance.

Second, even dissemination of information communicates trust and support. Followers tend to thrive in environments where there is open communication and the expectation of follower success. Insecurities develop when followers perceive leaders as inconsistent and selective in information sharing. When sharing information sporadically or unevenly, leaders communicate unreliability and perpetuate silos - division and contentiousness between departments. Followers vying for favorable positions with leaders often engage in unhealthy competition perpetuated by the withholding or rationing of information. Sharing knowledge and information with followers objectively ensures that followers have the tools needed to perform cooperatively and with confidence.

Third, clarity is essential in information sharing. Leaders communicate competence and stability when presenting information in a clear and concise fashion. When directions are vague and ambiguous, leaders saddle followers with the burden of trying to figure out what a leader wants. In a sense, the leader has laden the follower with the task of reading the leader's mind. Leaders voicing the expectation, "You should know what I would want," place inordinate pressure upon individual followers to think for two with one mind. This type of leader behavior is often typical in an iconic environment where the identity and personality of the organization are indistinguishable from those of the leader.

There is a certain arrogance attached to the thinking that followers should always be able to anticipate a leader's needs, desires, or responses to issues. This is not about lattes, office or project aesthetics. Habitual occurrences are, for most, easy to integrate over time, but ideas, strategies, and judgments are another story altogether. It is commendable, perhaps, when it happens that a follower can guess a leader's plan, but when thinking for another becomes an expectation, it creates undue pressure. Because of the power dynamic in the leader/follower relationship, a follower, who is hoping to please, may deny feeling pressured to think for her boss. All the while, though, the acquiescent follower silently nurses an ulcer at home.

Fourth, leaders convey confidence and trust when allowing followers the freedom and autonomy to accomplish goals and assignments without encumbrances. Responsibility and accountability without authority creates undo frustration for followers and communicates mistrust and leader perceptions of follower incompetence. Leaders put followers in an impossible situation when assigning tasks and impeding followers' abilities to achieve. Leaders hinder followers' success by withholding the resources or information needed to ensure task completion. Additionally, leaders thwart followers' abilities to perform, especially shared tasks, by withholding the support needed to ensure cooperation among all the persons needed to bring tasks to fruition. It is distressing, literally, for a follower to: (a) be assigned a cooperative task for which the follower is held ultimately responsible; (b) not get cooperation from others whose input is needed; and then (c) be held accountable for the inadequate outcome of the project. Far too often followers fall into disfavor with their leaders for the poor outcome of projects over which the follower has no real control. In the end, the failed task only confirms leader suspicions of incompetence on the part of the follower, whose only return for accepting a challenge is frustration caused by hindrances and inadequate support.

Fifth, availability communicates involvement, interest and support. Inaccessible leaders create particular difficulty for followers, especially when questions abound and no one is available to provide answers. When a leader is distracted or constantly multitasking, followers perceive the leader as being uninterested. Many a follower complain about leaders who are so busy and rushed all the time that they blurt out quick answers to questions followers have not had the chance to completely frame. There is a biblical proverb for this. *"He that answers a matter before he hears it, it is folly and shame to him."*[4]

Being dismissive toward followers communicates an air of superiority. When leaders refuse to invest the time and attention needed to fully answer or address follower concerns, followers are left to decipher bits and pieces of information and make decisions accordingly. Some of the most unavailable leaders impose the highest performance standards for followers. Generally, followers are seeking to meet, and for some, exceed the challenges given, but find it an impossible endeavor when leaders are too busy or impatient to assist when needed. Brenda is such a leader. Brenda's inaccessibility simply makes it difficult for followers to execute tasks without apprehension and tension. When a crisis arose that necessitated Brenda's immediate attention, rather than lend support, Brenda contemptuously admonished her staff for the interruption. As demonstrated by Brenda, mere physical presence does not communicate availability. Unfortunately, curt leaders tend to rationalize trivializing behavior as training or demonstrating confidence in followers' abilities to make independent decisions. Far too often, however, lost or slowed productivity, though attributed to follower deficiency, is also the result of hurried, unavailable leaders refusing become engaged and simply not listening.

Sixth, leaders who communicate forthrightly convey respect and appreciation for followers' work ethic. The impulsive and impatient leader communicates disregard for the worth and value of followers and their efforts to contribute to the organization. How often has a follower worked tirelessly on a project just to learn through a casual leader comment, "Oh that? I decided to go with something else. Didn't you know? I thought you knew." Additionally, when a leader assigns a specific task to a follower and then decides to reassign the task to another without informing the one to whom the assignment was first given, that follower feels taken for granted. Leaders could spare followers needless effort, not to mention, distress by communicating more directly.

Seventh, a respectful leader communicates value for the personhood of followers. Leaders who honor boundaries of appropriateness in their behaviors toward followers cultivate an environment of principled decision-making. When leaders conduct themselves presumptuously toward followers, leaders exploit the power dynamic in the leader/follower relationship. Aside from being belittling to followers, impertinent leader behavior is abusive. Audacious leaders often think their behavior should be taken in stride, but in actuality, these leaders exercise poor judgment and create apprehension in followers. Inappropriate leader behavior compromises leader integrity, that of followers and the organization.

Eighth, a unified leadership team communicates stability to followers. It is unlikely that all members of a leadership team will agree or enjoy congenial interactions all the time. However, respectful communications must be the standard in the presence of followers at all times. In addition to attempting to understand particular leader expectations, followers also have to learn to navigate through the discord that sometimes exists between individual leaders.

Leader conflict creates awkwardness for followers and often imposes upon followers to take stances of loyalty. The resulting disharmony obscures any former clarity with which followers were able to discern previously, and communication becomes tense and difficult between followers and any opposed leader. As well, leaders who disparage other leaders or followers in communications with followers communicate irresponsibility. Certain conversations are for peer groups and leaders and followers do not share that distinction.

One could argue the significance of benign interpretations of communication. The truth is leaders and followers are both more likely to respond to validating forms of communication than the opposite, and since every leader is also a follower in one way or another, the benefits can be mutual and cyclical. In this age of rapidly advancing technology, it is important to make the most of human interactions as they occur. What separates people from computers, for example, is the fact that people possess feelings and expectations that have the power to affect and predict productivity. Unlike computers or machinery, human beings have certain intrinsic needs that have to be met in order to perform at their best. A sobering reality to the staunch pragmatist is that follower unmet needs become barriers to performance. It is that simple. The return for thoughtful and conscientious communication brings value and worth to the effort.

What have the following individuals in common?

Wilhelm Steinitz (1886-1894), Austria-Hungary, United States

Emanuel Lasker (1894-1921), Germany

Jose Raul Capablanca (1921-1927), Cuba

Alexander Alekhine (1927-1935, 1937-1946), France, Russian émigré

Max Euwe (1935-1937), Netherlands

Mikhail Botvinnik (1948-1957, 1958-1960, 1961-1963), Soviet Union (Russia)

Vasily Smyslov (1957-1958), Soviet Union (Russia)

Mikhail Tal (1960-1961), Soviet Union (Latvia)

Tigran Petrosian (1963-1969), Soviet Union (Armenia)

Boris Spassky (1969-1972), Soviet Union (Russia)

Robert James "Bobby" Fischer (1972-1975), United States

Anatoly Karpov (1975-1985), Soviet Union (Russia)

Garry Kasparov (1985-2000), Soviet Union, Russia

Vladimir Kramnik (2000-2007), Russia

Viswanathan Anand (2007-current), India

You probably guessed right. They are world chess champions. Interestingly, their ages range from 22 years old to 58 during their reigns as masters of the game. The game of chess is considered to have originated near or about the second century in China. Still, most of its acclaim appears to have derived from the thought that India was the birthplace of the game of chess during the sixth century. From its earliest popularity in China, India, Persia, and Europe, chess evolved and spread throughout the continents over the centuries. Chess represented then, as it does now, a war game of sorts in which armies serve to gain and defend territory while every effort is made to capture the opposing army's king.

Any one of us who has attempted to learn or master the game of chess has encountered the methodology of the game. What makes playing chess well such a concentrated effort is the deliberation that has to go into every decision. In the game of chess, players have to not only attempt to execute their objectives but also to anticipate the interpretive thoughts and motives of the opposition. Chess players have to constantly consider how their individual moves will be perceived by their opponents. With the ultimate goal of subduing the other player's army and capturing the opposition's king, each player devises a strategy that comprises short-term and long-term goals.

Communication for leaders should be just as deliberate, measured, and purposeful as strategizing is for chess players. Leadership carries with it an understood and accepted level of authority, which adds significance and weight to a leader's words, actions, and behaviors. For that reason communication in leadership can make all the difference in making, breaking, mending, or destroying the leader/follower relationship. Verbal communication is the least weighty of the three forms of leader communication because words convey any number of thoughts and intentions. Even so, it takes action to consummate the spoken word. Speakers of any spectrum, whether it be political, commercial, industrial, or religious communicate to listeners with words. The spoken word can be helpful, encouraging, clarifying, or comforting. At the same time, the spoken word can cause hurt, confusion, instability, and alienation.

When a leader speaks with followers, the leader's words convey messages that transmit perceptions; one being self-perception and the other being the leader's perception of followers. Consider Tiberious McCarthan (pseudonym).

Tiberious is a general manager of a car dealership that has been grossing an average of 28% under cost each month for the past year. Turnover is high and employee morale is low. The strange thing about this is that consumer visits to the dealership is above average and notwithstanding the window shoppers who have no plans to buy, would be purchasers have been choosing to take their business elsewhere. The dealership owner asked me to ascertain the reasons for the high staff turnover, which he considered to be detrimental to the dealership's ability to establish a firm customer base. He also asked me to map out a plan of action that could help the dealership to retain its sales team and convince perusing customers to buy.

During my initial period of observation it became apparent to me that leadership communication and the discontinuity of the same were major contributing factors to the dealership's problems with staff and customers. For one, no two of the fifteen salespeople were on the same page. I could ask the same procedural question to personnel separately and receive any number of varied responses. Personnel also seemed to be confused about what was expected of them by different members of the management team.

The dealership, at the time, employed three managers, each of whom demonstrated a different leadership style. The assistant manager, Traci, employed a dictatorial style of leadership. Her supervisor, Bob, the operations manager, was more collaborative in his approach to decision-making; and then there was the general manager, Tiberious, who rarely communicated verbally with employees preferring instead to convey most information via memorandums.

Issues arose when, upon receiving a written directive from the general manager, Bob would seek consensus from the sales personnel while Traci would insist upon strict compliance from the same group and levy swift reprimands in response to any real or perceived resistance. The sales personnel were essentially receiving mixed messages from leadership. Firstly, the leaders created an atmosphere of confusion when, on the one hand, sales people were invited to participate in decision-making by the operations manager, and on the other, prevented from any participatory engagement by their immediate supervisor. Secondly, the sales personnel received mixed messages from leadership about their perceptions of followers. Tiberious, who rarely talked with the sales personnel, exhibited an aloofness that sent messages of disinterest, indifference, and reticence to employees while Bob, who sought consensus and collaboration, communicated value for the thoughts, ideas and opinions of workers. Adding to employees' confusion, the dictatorial Traci exemplified behavior that sent messages of perceived incompetence on the part of employees. Simmering mistrust had been brewing among the sales personnel who felt ignored by Tiberious, appreciated by Bob, but constrained by Traci. Needless to say, there were many lessons to be learned at the dealership about the significance of leader values and how they inform leader communication.

Consider the following practices of leaders who understand the importance of communicating thoughtfully with followers. To be effective requires only that a leader exerts influence, good or not. To qualify my use of effective here, I mean leaders whose communication strategies lead both followers and their organizations toward the realization of company or institutional goals.

⅃ **Effective leaders are like chess players who have learned to avoid making decisions in isolation.**

Chess players realize that every move communicates something of the thoughts, perceptions and objectives of the player who moves. What makes chess such a slow and methodical game is the deliberation players engage in pondering each and every move. Contemplative players ask themselves internally, "What will my move communicate? What will be my opponent's interpretation of my move and how will my opponent react based on her perception of my move? Will this move communicate a defense strategy or an offensive attack?"

Thoughtful leaders learn to engage in internal deliberation before acting or reacting. Effective leaders consider how followers will interpret their words, actions, or behaviors. Leader, Joyce Meyer, suggests that our individual tendency is to judge ourselves by our intentions while judging others based on their actions. It is important that leaders recognize that their words, actions, and behaviors may not always accurately convey their intentions. Have you ever spoken one thing only to have the listener hear something totally different? The listener will almost always judge the speaker's words, actions, and behaviors based on the listener's personal perceptions. Therefore, leaders must make every deliberate effort to think about how followers will interpret leader communications.

It is entirely possible that Tiberious' intention in formalizing every directive in memo form was to protect everyone from misunderstanding and to provide a reference for company expectations. Nonetheless, the employees interpreted his actions differently, especially since Tiberious used the memorandums as his primary method of communication with employees. The employees interpreted his constant memorandums as antagonistic and an affront to their collective and individual integrity. If Tiberious made a point to consider how employees might interpret his actions, he might have reconsidered his approach to communication. Tiberious could have spent time circulating among employees, sharing and listening to their concerns. It is likely that his memos may have been better received and become fewer as the need decreased with more verbal communication.

ℷ Effective leaders are like chess players who have learned to observe the expectations of others.

While individuals are unique, much of human behavior has been repeated over the centuries. People generally have in common the need to be heard, validated, valued, and appreciated. Bob understood his subordinates' needs to connect and participate in decision-making. The sales personnel felt affirmed by Bob because he demonstrated an inclusive approach to leadership. When Bob engaged the employees as colleagues and solicited their input the employees eagerly responded until their ideas were struck down by Traci. The sales personnel developed a sense of ownership and responsibility for the success of the company when they were treated with high regard.

ℷ Effective leaders are like chess players who spend time with other players of excellence.

Effective leaders learn not only to glean from the experiences of others but, in the development of close associations and friendships with outstanding leaders, new leaders can develop systems of accountability.

There is a biblical proverb that speaks well to this concept. *"As iron sharpens iron, a friend sharpens a friend."⁵* When leaders embrace the concept of transparency with other leaders, they are better able to realize the benefits of others' experiences. Power, which is an inherent component of leadership, can be intensely seductive and all leaders need ethical grounding. Tiberious, the general manager and Traci, the assistant manager operated in a vacuum, which perpetuated their individual autonomy. Both essentially alienated their subordinates and in so doing harmed the organization.

ℓ **Effective leaders exploit mentoring opportunities.**

The word, "mentor" originated from the mythological character named mentor who was the friend of the ancient Greek King Ulysses in Homer's Odyssey. At the king's request he took care of and became a personal and professional counselor and guide to the king's son while Ulysses was away.

Essentially, mentoring is training and developmental assistance provided by a senior colleague within or apart from a protégé's organization. Mentors provide knowledge and support by serving in such roles as colleague, teacher, coach, counselor, advocate, and role model. Individuals enter into mentoring relationships with varying expectations including career coaching, career assistance, and knowledge sharing. Mentoring has consistently been shown in studies to be the single most valuable element for a successful career. Individuals who participate in mentoring relationships inevitably enjoy the benefits of assisted personal and professional growth, which can facilitate the protégé's advancement in the organization.[6] Pauline, a human resources director, shared her experience as a protégé. "I had a mentor who helped to groom my educational and career path from the time I was in high school, through post graduate school. He guided me every step of the way and I believe I am where I am today as a result of his commitment to my development as a person."

Technological advances are contributing to the ease and flexibility of developing mentoring relationships without the need for proximity. James, a partner in a large legal firm, confirms this. "I currently mentor two junior lawyers straight out of law school and we communicate more by email and mobile phones than in person. We get together once a month for a long lunch, but with email and cell phones we touch base several times a week. It's great."

Internet communications present valuable work experiences that ultimately enhance mentoring relationships for protégés of companies that endeavor to establish borderless networking and communications. Birthed out of a concern for finding enough qualified workers among the young after the impending retirement of the baby boomer generation, IBM has commenced an initiative whereby they provide monetary incentives to older, seasoned company workers willing to provide online mentoring for young professionals.

Organizations today are not only incorporating new forms of mentoring to accommodate the values and expectations of younger workers, but also to benefit and enhance the organizational structure. Some organizations have begun to invest in professional consulting and coaching services to groom emerging executives for mutual benefit between the individual and the company. Val, a recruiter for a fortune 500 company talked about how her company has initiated coaching for senior leaders, who then, in turn, mentor middle managers. "We just decided to try to arrest issues of silos and burnout. Coaching for leaders is expensive, but it is worth the investment to bring out the best in our leaders. In the long run it saves the company money because we have less turf protecting among managers, but ultimately and most importantly, it benefits the customers."

Skillful leaders establish relationships with peers to whom they can be accountable. They place value on mentoring and personal development. Skillful leaders think deeply about decisions before implementation and recognize that investing valuable time and resources in empowering followers builds productive work teams that ultimately benefit their organizations. The managerial team at the car dealership gained valuable insights into how their individualized leadership choices created a chaotic atmosphere for workers. After much discussion, guidance, and introspection, the leaders were able to agree upon a systematic approach to meeting staff members' needs for value, inclusion, and consistency.

Workers Communicate To Customers, Oh Yes They Do!

Assertive workers in today's workforce have little reluctance when it comes to assessing whether they feel valued at a particular organization, especially workers who are highly skilled and educated.

As a customer of a few of the large commercial airlines, I often comment that I can distinguish those most pleasant for which to work. It is really quite simple. I notice that a certain company's employees are generally warm, relaxed, professional, and well groomed. While most airline employees may demonstrate one or a combination of the aforementioned characteristics, there are certain groups that appear to exhibit the characteristics most consistently. It has been my observation that companies that demonstrate value for their employees have a more loyal customer base as happy employees make for happy customers.

There are specific organizations that I know are difficult to work for because of how I observe their employees treat customers. Employees of antagonistic employers are often slovenly attired, curt, impatient, and disrespectful to customers. I often suggest to clients that all the efforts in the world to increase profits will fall short as long as their employees have to endure a hostile work environment. In antagonistic corporate cultures absenteeism, high turnover, silos, and infighting among group members never cease. People simply do not respond gleefully to environments that breed unfair competition, isolation, conflict, distrust, and suspicion. That is not to suggest that rules should not exist or that organizations should neglect to implement systems of checks and balances - to the contrary. There are ways, still, to cultivate an environment of professionalism and high expectations without engendering resentment. Resentful employees have ways of getting back at their employers. One way is by communicating their displeasure to customers.

I walked into a well-known department store a few months ago after deciding to purchase a wax treatment for my kitchen floor. I approached an employee to ask for advice on the best product to purchase. This employee was apparently not happy with his employer. He suggested that I should purchase the treatment in the blue container, but that I should make the purchase at another store, which he named. He stated that the competitor's prices were much better.

On another occasion, I attempted to rent a car at a busy southeast airport. It seemed that my online reservation could not be found in the system and I had to start from the beginning. When the representative quoted the price for a three-day rental as $100 more per day than my original online quote, I turned to my traveling companions and commented, "That seems to be pretty expensive." The representative, to whom I was not speaking, retorted, "Well, if you don't like it, call Hertz or Avis if you think their prices are better." I suppose she noticed my flabbergasted expression and continued, "I have their numbers and will gladly call them for you, or if you like, here is the phone, speak to them yourself!" With that, the representative placed her employer's desk telephone on top of the counter and began dialing her company's competitor on the spot.

That employee's behavior was comical to me, but not so at all to her employer. Although that worker's superior apologized and upgraded our rental, neither I nor any of my traveling companions has returned to conduct business with that company since. It has been over five years. It is not as though we purpose to avoid this particular company, it just no longer comes to mind. When I think of renting a car now, I think of other agencies, including the ones the previous company's representative had suggested so emphatically and offered to call for us - on her employer's telephone no less.

Employers need to recognize that workers are their first line of interaction with customers. There is simply no way to monitor all of the interactions employees have with customers. Recording telephone conversations "for accuracy and quality purposes" is a costly attempt to circumvent a problem from a watchdog perspective. When employees feel valued most can likely be trusted.

I was in a major commercial bank (whose most recent quarterly profits exceeded 2.5 billion dollars, by the way) when I overheard this conversation between a customer and a teller.

Customer, "Good morning, I would like to cash my payroll check."
Teller, "Do you have an account with us?
Customer, "No I don't, but here is my ID".
Teller, "Do you have an account with us?
Customer, "No. I do not, but I have my driver's license and other ID."
Teller, "Would you like to open an account with us?
Customer, "No. Not right now. I just want to cash my check."
Teller, "That will be $10.00"
Customer, "Why? I have ID"
Teller, "Because you don't have an account with us, I have to charge you $10.00"
Customer, "But the check is drawn on your bank!"
Teller, "Sir, I know it is. But, if you want, you can open an account right now. It should only take a few minutes. Otherwise, if you do not have an account, I have to charge you $10.00 to cash your check"
Customer, "My check is only a few dollars. It's from my part-time job and it is your own check from your depositor!"
Teller, "I'm sorry sir. Do you want to open an account?"
Customer, "No."
Teller, "Well, what do you want to do?"
Customer, "I'll pay the $10.00."

By the way, as long as there are people who will pay the coercive fees, institutions will continue to charge. My father describes this evolving tendency as, "whatever the market will bear."

Everyone could tell that the teller did not agree with the bank's policy and was no less sympathetic to the customer than were onlookers. In fact, the teller appeared embarrassed to have to convey such a coercive policy. It is perhaps true that the bank has much to offer depositors. However, the teller mentioned not one benefit the potential depositor could expect from establishing an account with that bank. The only message the teller communicated with the customer was to join the company or be penalized. Companies and institutions develop any number of incentives and account benefits for potential and existing clientele. Yet, when coercion and intimidation become part of the selling points, workers become the faces behind companies' *true* values.

Unhappy workers, no matter how highly trained, find it difficult to pretend loyalty, especially when unmonitored.

A highly decorated sales manager for one of the largest retailers in the country states, "The greedier my company gets and the more they try to take from me, the more determined I am to learn all I can and make as many friends out of customers and would be customers as possible so that I can take my skill and client base someplace where I will be appreciated!"

Getting back to the bank, here is a potential depositor who, by his own statement, works two jobs. His part-time wage was only $89.00 and for refusing to become a depositor on the spot, the bank took $10.00 of that (this, again, from a bank that boasts quarterly net profits in excess of 2.5 billion dollars). Whether or not the customer was a depositor elsewhere and could have simply deposited his check is immaterial. Since when should potential depositors be pressured into opening an account or punished for not engaging a relationship with any institution?

Not only was it apparently worth it to the customer to pay nearly 8% of his wage to not become a depositor of that bank, but he left there feeling angry and cheated. He determined to share his experiences with others and never return. On a positive note, if that customer is not a depositor at another bank already, this experience may inspire him to consider opening an account someplace. I am willing to bet $10.00, all the same, that it will not be you know where.

DIVERSITY COMMUNICATES
APPRECIATION

The face of the American workforce is evolving to reflect a changing demographic. The American workforce is now populated with more women and people of varying ethnic backgrounds and cultures than ever before. This trend will likely continue at a rapid pace. Not only must organizations pursue diversity efforts in an effort toward equity and opportunity, but also to demonstrate acceptance and appreciation beyond mere tolerance. To say that an individual or group is the object of tolerance is no longer politically or socially correct. Contemporary workers are not only less concerned about assimilation but disdain being tolerated. Twenty-first century employees are more concerned about being appreciated for the unique talents, beliefs, and backgrounds they bring to organizational culture than being a statistic that satisfies quotas. No longer can companies ignore this fact or marginalize efforts toward genuine inclusion. Leaders of progressive organizations will remain mindful of the shared space between the worker and the customer. Companies, to succeed, must be perceived by the public as respectful and appreciative of diversity and multiculturalism. Successful diversity initiatives not only promote acceptance and inclusion but also utilize differences for the benefit of organizational growth and gain.

Diversity is, in a word, variety. There are a variety of workers in today's workforce, consisting of various ethnicities and cultures, including the disabled, various age groups, people with various skill levels, the highly educated, the undereducated, and people with diverse spiritual beliefs. Multiculturalism is the integrating and inclusion of individuals of different ethnicities, cultures, religions, or nationalities. Organizational initiatives designed to encourage diversity communicate messages of appreciation to potential workers and once aboard, these workers will perform well and remain loyal to their employer. According to Gallop, organizational commitments to diversity directly influence workers' satisfaction and dedication to the company.[7] Promoting diversity is an investment that is certain to yield appreciative economic returns while attracting and retaining the best talent, which, in itself, contributes to competitive advantage.

While many companies have incorporated diversity initiatives in their organizational strategic thinking and planning, the challenge of implementation still confronts a number of company leaders. Unfortunately, some embrace a narrow perception of diversity as nothing more than affirmative action with the same agenda. Authentic diversity initiatives, however, are broader in scope than affirmative action and focus beyond issues of race and gender acceptance. This broader definition of diversity enables leaders to focus on developing workers' full potential because it takes into account internal factors that extend beyond obvious differences in appearance to include differences in capabilities, company roles, tenure, and personal characteristics. Resulting from past legislation regarding affirmative action, many companies may have implemented some degree of hiring strategy aimed at protecting themselves against lawsuits or public disapproval. Notwithstanding all the controversial legal and political strategizing surrounding inclusion on all fronts, authentic diversity initiatives celebrate, pursue, and applaud differences and this goes beyond doing just what is required. Open communication about diversity, especially between leaders and followers, promotes and encourages inclusion and engagement in the workplace. Organizations and their leaders must seek to create work environments that move beyond tolerance to respect, celebration, and appreciation for the uniqueness and value that various groups bring to the table. Diversity initiatives must reflect organizations' commitments in practical, observable ways. Companies that genuinely value diversity actively promote efforts to encourage its representation at all levels.

Authentic efforts toward equity and inclusion can be threatening to individuals whose personal values do not include an appreciation for differences among people. Diversity initiatives, to be successful, must be authentic. If not, resistance and resentment are bound to surface. When companies seek beyond mere representation to deliberately locating, hiring, and retaining the best talent, diversity initiatives become effective. Company leaders must look honestly at the effectiveness of their current diversity initiatives because change begins with the recognition that it is necessary. Authentic diversity goes beyond mere representation to fairness. It is when companies actively pursue methods to demonstrate appreciation for diversity that workers and community members recognize organizations' effort as sincere.

The Home Depot, for example, dedicates 23 million hours per year to diversity training and Sears holdings has put a mentoring program in place as part of its diversity initiative.[8] As many successful diversity endeavors have already demonstrated, investing resources into developing and perfecting viable diversity initiatives reflect a firm commitment that extends beyond mere trade.

WHAT'S CULTURE GOT TO DO WITH IT?

Organizations whose leaders aspire to establish or maintain a viable global presence must help their leaders develop the cultural competency skills required for a multinational environment. Cultural competence entails demonstrating knowledge and respect for the differences in beliefs, preferences, traditions, and values of various groups of people. Cross-cultural communication implies the receiving and sharing of information between individuals or groups from varying backgrounds, beliefs, or societal structures. Culturally competent leaders demonstrate the skills needed to work with various ethnic groups and the attitude of wanting to do so effectively.

Cross-cultural leadership communication begins with an understanding of culture. Culture is the lens through which people see the world around them as it relates to informing their values, beliefs, religious norms and place in society. While communication is the process of sending and receiving messages, effective communication is defined by that which is equally fruitful and rewarding to both the sender and receiver of information. Miscommunication occurs when information processes are thwarted by a lack of understanding by the sender, the receiver, or both. Because knowledge of culture is so valuable in the global environment, leaders should learn to interpret what is unspoken as well as that which is clearly articulated. Knowledge of what is unsaid can enlighten leaders as to how to utilize language in its proper framework. Significant non-verbal communication spans across international and linguistic boundaries. Leaders who master non-verbal communication will be more likely to function effectively in the cross-cultural arena.

Anthropologist, Edward T. Hall, asserts that communication is more about context than information itself.[9] As Hall points out, all information in all cultures is processed through the lens of context. Hall's concepts of polychronic and monochronic cultures and high-context verses low-context cultures yield valuable insight into deciphering cultural patterns. Hall defines a polychronic culture as a culture in which people value, and hence practice, engaging in several activities and events at the same time. [10] Polychronic cultures value flexibility, collaboration, and building long-term relationships. Monochronic cultures are more linear in that people prefer to manage one activity at a time.[11] Monochronic cultures tend to value personal space, short-term surface acquaintances with business associates, regimentation, and bureaucracy.

Hall's cultural vocabulary may appear technical and complicated at first but with time and a little practice, leaders can grasp the meanings of each distinction. The prefix, "poly" has to do with plurality and "mono" refers to singularity. "Chronic" describes a habit or behavior that persists over time. According to Hall, the United States would be considered a monochronic culture. In US culture, most people prefer to engage in one activity at a time. For example, it is considered rude to answer telephone calls during dinner or multi-task during a meeting. Americans tend to expect people to devote their undivided attention to the project at hand rather than to participate in another activity at the same time. Conversely, in a polychronic culture like Nigeria, it is not uncommon for meeting facilitators to undertake several activities at once, including answering telephone calls and giving unrelated instructions to administrative assistants during a business meeting.

In US culture, people tend to keep business associates at a distance when it comes to social interaction. That again is about being singularly focused. Quite the reverse is customary in a polychronic culture like Brazil where people expect to interact socially with business colleagues. Americans tend to shy away from inquisitiveness from co-workers who are interested in their personal lives unless there is some mutual interest. On the other hand, in Brazil, people gladly share information about their personal lives and expect others to as well. In US culture, people deal with the business at hand and keep it formal for the most part. Yet in Brazil, the lines between business dealings and social interactions often intersect. One reason for this is that trust is paramount in developing business relationships with colleagues in polychronic cultures like Nigeria and Brazil. In order to establish trust, members of these cultures tend to want to know with whom they are doing business before sealing a contract. Brazilians want to know about a potential business associate's background and family. Whereas, in US culture, trust matters, but only so far as there is written confirmation to protect everyone's interests. For the most part, Americans tend to establish business relationships based on mutually agreed upon terms and systems of accountability.

In formal meetings, Americans tend to get right down to business after a greeting and lighthearted opening. This is true even in conducting telephone exchanges. "Hello, may I please speak with Bob?" Conversely, in South Africa, business meetings may begin with everyone greeting each other and engaging in several minutes of conversation about each other's well-being, background, and family all before any formal discourse begins. When calling the home of a South African colleague, it is considered brass to simply say, "Hello," and ask for someone else by name. The proper greeting consists of taking a few minutes to engage the person who answers the telephone about their well-being and that of their family. During the course of the extended greeting, the listener clues the caller when it is polite to ask to speak to the person of interest.

While the concepts relating to understanding cultural differences may appear technical, learning about cultural nuances can be quite enjoyable. Aside from the complicated vernacular, two of the most basic differences between cultures is how people view time and space. In US culture, time is considered a valuable commodity of which everyone has a limited amount. Remember this? "Hurry, time is of the essence!" How about this one? "Time is money!" In some African cultures and Latin American cultures, time is seen as relative and subjective.

Once, on a business trip to South America, some local friends and I made plans to go to the beach. We set the time for 9AM the following morning. I was up and dressed by 8:30 and found myself seated in the living room wondering if my hosts had forgotten all about our day trip. At approximately 11:15, my friends arose from sleep, greeted me gleefully and casually waltzed into the kitchen to have breakfast and prepare a big lunch for our outing. It was all I could do to keep from laughing myself under the couch to consider that 9AM really meant 9AM in parts of South America. After calling and inviting friends and relatives near and far, my friends prepared to leave. After a few stops along the way, we finally arrived at the beach at 3:30 in the afternoon. It was great!

Hall's research on proxemics, which has to do with proximity, describes cultural differences as they relate to the view and use of space. When it comes to personal space, cultures tend to differ vastly. In Japan, for example, it is not uncommon for grown children to remain at home until married. In many African cultures, it is expected that young women will go from their parents' homes directly to that of their husbands. In US culture, people want their own space. Grown children move out of their parents' homes and into homes of their own. In fact, it is not uncommon for some American parents to encourage their grown, unmarried children to branch out on their own. They liken it to the eagle pushing its young from the nest.

Hall further explains that polychronic cultures tend to be part of a high context domain, while monochronic cultures tend to be part of a low context domain. In high context cultures, information surrounding a message comes from the context in which it is transmitted rather than from the message itself, whereas in low context cultures, most of the information is contained in the message. [12] In high-context cultures, like Japan, China, Korea Thailand, certain African, and Latin American countries, background information is implicit, and much of the message is carried in how the words relate to unspoken information. [13] Individuals in high-context cultures use expressive manner or non-verbal language such as voice, posture, gesture, body language, facial expression, and periods of silence in their communication. In low-context cultures, like the United States, Canada, Switzerland, and Germany, background information must be explicitly expressed because most of the message is carried by the words themselves, not by the context in which the words are expressed.

Hall contends that more information is transmitted in monochronic/low context cultures than in polychronic/high context cultures, but more information is shared in the polychronic than in the monochronic cultures.[14]

Hall's Monochronic and Polychronic Cultures

Work Categories	Monochronic	Polychronic
	Examples include: The United States, Northern Europe / Scandinavia, and Germany	Examples include: The Mediterranean nations, Latin America, and parts of Africa
Interpersonal Relations	Interpersonal relations are subordinate to present schedule	Present schedule is subordinate to Interpersonal relations
Activity Coordination	Schedule coordinates activity; appointment time is rigid.	Interpersonal relations coordinate activity; appointment time is flexible
Task Handling	One task at a time	Many tasks are handled simultaneously
Temporal Structure	Time is inflexible; time is tangible	Time is flexible; time is fluid
Work and personal time separability	Work time is clearly separable from personal time	Work time is not clearly separable from personal time
Organizational Perception	Activities are isolated from organization as a whole; tasks are measured by output in time (activity per hour or minute)	Activities are integrated into organization as a whole; tasks are measured as part of overall organizational goal

Source: Hall, Edward T. The Silent Language. New York: Anchor Books, 1973.

High-Context and Low-Context Cultures

<u>High Context Cultures</u>

Japan

Arab Countries

Greece

West Africa

Latin America

Spain

Italy

<u>Low Context Cultures</u>

England

France

North America

Scandinavian Countries

German-speaking Countries

Source: Hall, Edward T. The Silent Language. New York: Anchor Books, 1973.

Suppose it is lunchtime and you are walking past your colleague's desk. Everyone else has left for lunch and you ask your colleague, "Are you going for lunch?" In US culture, it is not uncommon for people to blatantly ask for what they want. Your colleague (whom you know reasonably well) responds, "I would love to but I am short a few dollars. Why don't you buy me lunch today and I will repay you tomorrow?" In Japan, your colleague might respond more like this: "It would be good to have a meal now, but I have much work to complete." The listener has to take the cue to invite the colleague to lunch. Your response could be, "I am going to the seafood restaurant for lunch right now and I know you are busy, may I ask you to please join me as my guest? It should not take long." In this way, your colleague gets to "save face." That is, you have spared him the embarrassment of telling you that he is hungry and has no money. In Japanese culture, protecting one's dignity and that of others is of very high importance. Japanese culture expects people to be gentle with each other's feelings, especially in person-to-person social interaction. Even when the answer for a favor is "no", the Japanese may still say "yes," and the listener has to interpret the denial by the delay in materializing the favor. In the end, it is as though the granter somehow still intends to bring the favor to pass.

The direct confrontation that characterizes communication in US culture is sometimes viewed as brazen and undignified by other cultures. Communication in US culture is more about the words that are spoken than the context surrounding the conversation. "Say what you mean and mean what you say." Conversely, in Japan, communication is more about the context and the listener has to pick up on what is not said. In Japan it might seem as though one is having two conversations at once, one with words and one that is unspoken.

Global leaders can develop cross-cultural competency and improve cross-cultural communication skills by developing flexibility. Flexibility and adaptability allow leaders to vacillate between cultural traditions and expectations without requiring change or creating uneasiness on the part of those with whom the leader interacts. Flexibility allows leaders to maintain amenable relations cross-culturally by alleviating tendencies toward placing negative value judgments on the actions and work ethics of others. Leaders who understand cultural differences can often circumvent the consequences of unintentional conflict.

There are two main considerations for leaders looking to improve their cross-cultural communication skills. The first is to recognize that cross-cultural communication begins with an appreciation of societal contexts. It is imperative that leaders understand cultural mores as a prerequisite for interpreting meaning in interpersonal communications. Secondly, leaders should consider the works of Hall, for example, to determine the specific characteristics that dominate various cultures.

Low-context and High-context Cultural Variations

Low-Context Culture	High-Context Culture
1. Overtly displays meanings through direct communication forms	1. Implicitly embeds meanings at different levels of the socio-cultural context
2. Values individualism	2. Values group sense
3. Tends to develop transitory personal relationship	3. Tends to take time to cultivate and establish a permanent personal relationship
4. Emphasizes linear logic	4. Emphasizes spiral logic
5. Values direct verbal interaction and is less able to read nonverbal expressions	5. Values indirect verbal interaction and is more able to read nonverbal expressions
6. Tends to use "logic" to present ideas	6. Tends to use more "feeling" in expression
7. Tends to emphasize highly structured messages, give details, and stress words and technical signs	7. Tends to give simple, ambiguous, non-contexting messages

Source: Hall, Edward T. The Silent Language. New York: Anchor Books, 1973.

A thorough understanding of one's own cultural framework will likely provide a leader with the foundational tools for proper inquiry into others' cultural frameworks. Leaders who accept responsibility for investigating and engaging culture on a deeper cognitive level will succeed in developing and improving their cross-cultural communication skills. As the global marketplace grows flatter, organizations that invest in preparing their leaders to develop cultural competence relative to the significant differences in cultural patterns may realize a competitive advantage over those who do not. Leaders have to take into consideration the effect of globalism on their teams and be prepared to adjust accordingly. Sometimes, this may mean investing in education, including learning other cultures and languages.

Globally, the use of language extends beyond face-to-face encounters into the virtual environment. The advent of the virtual office makes communication via technology more commonplace than in-person meetings, especially with differing time zones. Both formal language instruction and immersion can serve as viable organizational investments in developing the cultural competence necessary to foster relationships across national borders.

LEADING A SAMPLE
MULTICULTURAL TEAM

Leading a multicultural team requires the willingness to learn about each of the cultures represented. Here is a very brief introduction to three cultures along with suggestions for establishing cohesion in a team comprised of individuals representing the United States, Brazil, and Nigeria.

United States' Culture

The United States of America is a federal constitutional republic made up of fifty states, one federal district, and several territories. The United States has a population of over 300,000,000 people. A largely diverse nation, America consists of 75% percent Caucasian, 12.5% Latino, 12⅓% African American, 3.6% Asian, and .7% Native American.[15] The national language of the United States is English.

The United States functions under a democratic, secular form of government that embraces free market capitalism and the ideology of "separation between church and state." The most widely held religion in the United States is Christianity. Over seventy-five percent of the American population identifies as Christian. The remaining twenty-five percent comprise various forms of religious beliefs and expressions like Judaism, Hinduism, Islam, Buddhism, and others. In the United States, people often determine social class by the type of vocation or work one performs.

The concept of individualism bears significant footing in American culture. Americans embrace the notion that success is almost entirely linked to individual initiative, personal achievement, independence, and self-reliance. At work, Americans enjoy opportunities for autonomy and self-determination. One's position in American society is determined by one's own achievements as more so than status or age.

Americans typically do not display physical affection toward casual acquaintances or coworkers. Americans, as a rule, prefer not to establish personal relationships with business associates, as they value parameters between business and personal interactions. Americans favor building solid business relationships without personal familiarity as it conflicts with American values for privacy and physical space. Americans enjoy learning other languages but may not feel the need to learn another's language, especially for doing business in America or with an American company.

At work, Americans expect and adhere to a strict system of punctuality in business. The typical worker in the United States works an average of forty-three hours per week while those in leadership positions may work fifty or more hours per week. United States' corporate business culture includes business attire although casual "dress down" apparel has become gradually more acceptable. In the United States, organizations are largely geared toward corporate image. United States' corporate culture embraces a hard driving and achievement oriented ethos where management motivates workers through mechanisms of reward and punishment.

Brazilian Culture

The Federative Republic of Brazil comprises 26 states and 5,564 municipalities. Brazil functions under a democratic form of government and Brazilian law is based on Roman-Germanic tradition of civil law precepts. Brazil is the largest and most densely inhabited country in Latin America, and the fifth largest in the world in both land area and population. Brazil has a diverse population of nearly 185,000,000 people consisting of 54% Europeans, 38% multiracial, 6% Africans, .5% Asian, 1.1% Amerindian, and other indigenous Tupi and Guarani people. The national language of Brazil is Portuguese.

The main religion in Brazil is Roman Catholicism. About 74% of the Brazilian population identify themselves as Roman Catholics. Brazil has the largest population of Roman Catholics worldwide. Fifteen percent of the Brazilian population is protestant, 7% claim to be agnostics, and the remaining 4% practice a variety of religions including, Spiritism, Judaism, Buddhism, and Islam. In Brazil, people often determine social class by such economic indicators as vocation, residency, and education choices.

Socially, Brazilians are community oriented and engaging. In business interactions, Brazilians expect to develop personal relationships with colleagues and could appear overly inquisitive to non-Brazilians. While it is not required, Brazilians tend to demonstrate respect and appreciation for business associates who greet and converse with them in Portuguese.

Brazilian organizations are largely hierarchal and operate on a project-oriented system where responsibility rests with the employee to meet deadlines. Employees will generally stay for as long as it takes to complete tasks. Brazilian companies typically function in various locations and business travel is expected of employees. Leaders in Brazilian corporations often speak English and are largely multilingual. Overall, Brazilian corporate culture consists of highly qualified and experienced individuals in an extremely competitive, technologically up-to-date, and dynamic environment. Brazilians expect punctuality in business from visitors, but may themselves casually arrive past the designated time for meetings. In business encounters, Brazilians expect smart dress of suits and ties.

Nigerian Culture

The Federal Republic of Nigeria is a country in West Africa consisting of 36 state governments and 774 local government administrations. The Nigerian government functions as a federal republic based on English common law, Islamic law, and traditional law. Nigeria is the most densely populated country in Africa with a population of approximately 120,000,000 people.

Nigeria has over 250 different ethnic groups. The three largest are the Hausa-Fulani at 29%, the Yoruba at 21%, and the Igbo at 18%. The official language of Nigeria is English. There are also three main indigenous languages, which are Hausa, Igbo, and Yoruba. Fifty percent of the Nigerian population practice Islam, 40% practice Christianity, and 10% practice indigenous traditional religions. In Nigeria, economic power and wealth determine social status. Nigeria is a patriarchal society, where men largely dominate women and where women hold less social and professional status.

Socially, Nigerians are community oriented and engaging like Brazilians. Nigerians interact through physical touch (with the right hand only, with both hands, or by hugging. The left hand is considered reserved for personal utilities and therefore unclean). Greetings are of primary importance in Nigeria, as is respect for elders.

Nigerian business culture is largely hierarchal and is comparatively laid back to that of the United States. Rigor, competitiveness, and smart dress exist in Nigerian business while friendliness and community characterize the overall Nigerian corporate culture. Nigerians expect punctuality in business from visitors, but may casually arrive past the designated time for meetings. Nigerians conduct business matters in person and seek to develop personal relationships with business associates.

69

Recommendations for Leading a Multicultural Team

In leading a multicultural team comprised of individuals from the aforementioned three cultures, a leader may encounter behaviors and expectations that are conflicting, yet relative to the distinctions of each. These include issues in business and social etiquette. In forming global business relationships, a global leader must learn to address protocols related to business, social customs, and general decorum for each culture.

A culturally competent leader should offer extensive educational training about each of the represented cultures to the group and consider the following recommendations for managing a multicultural team comprised of Americans, Brazilians, and Nigerians.

1) Engage in practical exercises that offer practice opportunities for business and casual interactions for each culture.

2) Train the group to adhere to business and social protocols regarding the use of personal space in the United States, and likewise for Brazil and Nigeria.

3) Representatives from each culture should take turns educating and leading the group in acceptable social and business dining behaviors and practices.

4) Allow members of the group to lead and train others in the protocols of dress, as well as social and formal greeting techniques.

5) Lead fluidity exercises that emphasize adaptability and flexibility. For example, conduct exercises that include variations of venue, like scheduling and meeting clients for early morning meetings in the United States, lunch meetings in Brazil, and afternoon meetings in Nigeria.

6) Train members to practice communicating and scheduling meetings in America electronically, verses face-to-face encounters in Brazil and Nigeria.

Global leadership opportunities are vast and insight gained into corporate and cultural protocols can help to facilitate and enhance leader communication in developing business relationships.

As leaders and followers become more connected through mobile devices, less time will be spent in face to face encounters. Meetings will increasingly take place via video conference tools and in online platforms where attendees join and make their individual contribution at convenient times. It is imperative that leaders begin to observe and implement communication strategies that preserve the human need to be heard, understood, and valued. Effective communication is the key to establishing, building and cultivating lasting and meaningful relationships in business and beyond.

THE DYNAMIC OF

SPIRITUALITY

SPIRITUAL HUNGER AT WORK

Today's younger workers, with their differing values and assertive spirituality, are entering the workforce in significant numbers. Retiring baby boomers that initially took orders and prioritized work over family or personal time eventually paved the way for collaboration and inclusion, but are now being replaced by workers with an even broader cultural mindset. The twenty-first century workforce has a set of values that prioritize family, friendships, and community over work. It is not uncommon for today's workers to leave the office to attend school functions for their children or to supervise field trips. Family leave is becoming, at the same time, more popular as contemporary employees decide to start or enlarge their families mid-career.

It appears that today's workers are less loyal to jobs than were previous generations. Contemporary workers are confident in their skills and think little of gaining knowledge and experience and moving on. The loss of loyalty to employers is partially due to the current generation's witness of the decades of the eighties when massive layoffs and downsizings tainted the corporate image. While growing up, contemporary workers observed as their parents, who sacrificed plays, afterschool games, recitals, and family outings, were let go with no hesitation by the company for which they had sacrificed precious family time. Millennials (members of generation Y, especially) upon this observation, decided right then that they would prioritize life and family over work. In addition to the cost of memories left unmade, there is the nagging insecurity of suspecting that all the while one is working, one's employer is looking for ways to eliminate one's job.

Spiritual fulfillment speaks to the general well-being that individuals experience at work. According to my research, when workers experience spiritual fulfillment at work the likelihood for employee retention rises. Workers today perceive appreciation, inclusion, participative leadership, and respect for personal values as viable components that aid spiritual fulfillment. Spirituality at work also means allowing individuals to express their personal values and beliefs and have them respected by leadership. Personal fulfillment and contentment at work are different from spirituality in that spirituality expresses a person's core individual values. People today want and perhaps need to be able to share aspects of their lives that, in years past, would have been forbidden at work. Because work is so embedded in individuals' lives today, spirituality has to be also.

I make the case for organizational approaches to spirituality because of the prevalence of spiritual hunger among workers. The population in general has been expressing deep spiritual hunger over the past decades, especially since the late 80's. Alienation on a societal scale appears to have resulted from emaciated social values.[16] The so-called, dot-com bust, massive layoffs, downsizings, and bank failures of the 90's perpetuated a sobering search for meaning in the populous at-large. Attendance at church and other religious activities increased as the gods of money, greed, and profligacy failed to satisfy the most innate of human longings. Families torn apart by skyrocketing divorce rates found little solace in tangibles and people began looking for something intangible and even divine to believe in. The pursuit of spiritual fulfillment became about people looking for significance in their lives.

People began, in greater numbers, to publicize their need for answers to questions like:

* Why am I here?

* Why was I created?

* What is my purpose in life?

* Is there more to life than this?

* Is this all there is?

* Am I fulfilling my purpose in life by working on this job?

* What am I gaining from this experience?

* Do I matter to my employer?

* Do I matter to my supervisor?

* Does my employer care about me as an individual?

* Do my needs matter here?

* Are my needs being fulfilled at this job?

* Should I stay here?

* Am I appreciated here?

* Do my opinions count here?

* When I leave this earth, will it matter that I
  was here?

In light of the implications of the aforementioned ponderings, organizational leaders need to realize that a mere pat on the back for a job well done leaves much to be desired when it comes to cultivating an environment of spiritual fulfillment. Spiritual hunger within the society as a whole may be well evidenced by the plethora of psychic venues and advertisements that flood the media. People are looking for answers, for connection, and for purpose. While an organizational approach to spirituality may appear to be a tall order for companies, especially given the diversity among staff, which include non-believers on all levels, the first step is to reconcile the fact that spirituality is not about religion. Spirituality is about workers' search for meaning in their lives. Spirituality is about self-actualization.

Notwithstanding the fact that many individuals engage religion in their search for meaning and purpose; organizations can contribute to workers' spiritual fulfillment through formal and informal mechanisms that address workers' needs apart from or inclusive of religious activities.

WORKER SPIRITUALITY

Spiritually hungry workers inform the need for organizational approaches to spirituality. In a recent survey to explore workers' attitudes about spirituality and work, I confirmed correlations between spiritual fulfillment and job satisfaction. Global inferences were evidenced by participation from respondents representing the United States and six nations in South America, Africa, Europe and the Pacific Islands.

The participants were between the ages of eighteen and fifty-six. Fifty-six percent of the participants held bachelor degrees. Thirty-eight percent had completed some graduate or postgraduate studies. Six percent of the participants described themselves as high school graduates with no undergraduate studies. The research pool consisted of individuals who are of a variety of faiths, as well as agnostics, and non-believers in religion. Here are some of the survey findings.

Fewer than half of the participants surveyed describe themselves as happily employed. Nearly a fifth described themselves as employed but looking for work elsewhere and just over one-in-ten described themselves as employed and unhappy at work. To a question of whether participants planned to remain with their current employers, nine-in-ten indicated a desire or plans to leave within one or two years. These findings indicate that nearly six-in-ten or 60% of workers are dissatisfied on their jobs. This finding is consistent with the indications of the Institution of Management and Administration's (IMOA) 2005 report on employee satisfaction.[17]

Employment Status

- Happily employed

- Unhappily employed

- Unhappily employed with definite plans to leave current employer within 1 or 2 years

- Unhappily employed and open to new opportunities from a new employer

- Unhappily employed with no plans to leave

87%

56%

44%

16%   12%

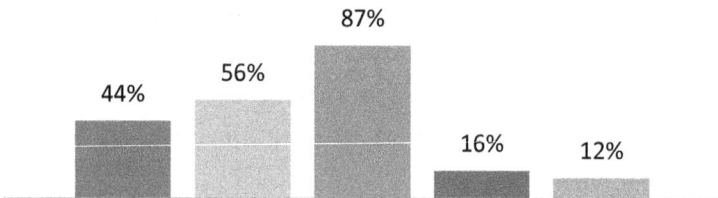

(More than half of the participants surveyed express being unhappy at work and more than half of those are planning to leave their current employers)

According to the IMOA report, employee dissatisfaction has been steadily mounting since 1995 when four-in-ten of workers expressed dissatisfaction with their jobs compared with the report's 2005 finding of half.

My research indicated that nine of every ten participants had expectations of developing friendships and other personal relationships at work. According to medical director and family therapist, J. Lebron McBride, the development of meaningful relationships at work helps to cultivate an environment of community, which can be beneficial to employers because people who consider themselves as members of a communal relationship tend not to be inclined toward negativity in the workplace.[18]

In the interest of community, over half of the participants indicated a desire for work to be an extension rather than a separate part of their lives.

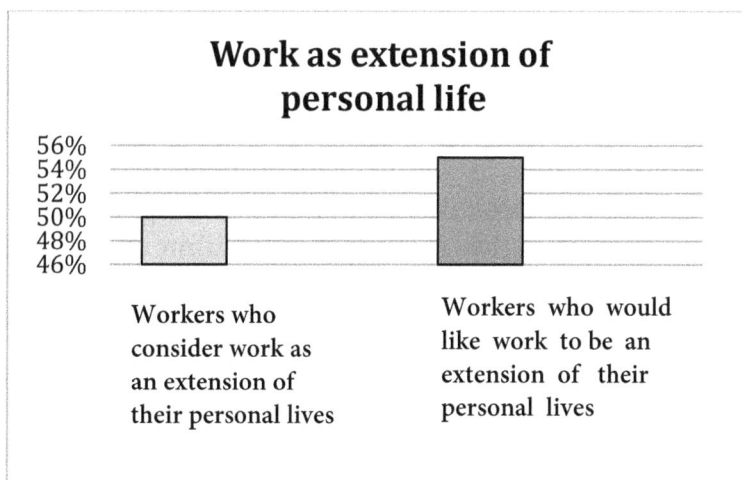

Work as extension of personal life

56%	
54%	
52%	
50%	
48%	
46%	

Workers who consider work as an extension of their personal lives

Workers who would like work to be an extension of their personal lives

It is notable that workers who find meaning in both their work and personal lives experience general well-being and inner satisfaction more than workers who find meaning only in their personal lives.[19] Nearly eight-in-ten participants indicated a desire to participate in decision-making at work. Seven-in-ten expressed a desire to participate in company planning. The desire to participate in decision-making and planning at work correlates to the endeavor to achieve personal satisfaction on the job and to feel contributory to positive outcomes.

Desire for inclusion

- Desire to participate in company decision-making
- Desire to participate in company planning

Workers seek inclusion and meaningful participation for spiritual fulfillment

To clarify the issue of spirituality as it relates to religion, participants were asked to describe themselves in either category. Fewer than half of the participants surveyed characterized themselves as "religious." The participants' definitions of religious varied from the belief in God to a personal routine of religious practice. Nearly seven-in-ten of the participants described themselves as "spiritual." Participants' definitions of spiritual included having an acknowledgment of God and a strong sense of self. Half of the participants described themselves as being both religious and spiritual.

Given a list from which to select all that apply to participants' personal values, spirituality, or religious beliefs, seven-in-ten listed "demonstrating love and obedience to God," while nine-in-ten indicated that demonstrating love for fellow human beings applies to their personal values, spirituality, or religious beliefs. More than half also pointed to self-sacrifice as pertaining to their personal values while six-in-ten included respecting other people's values and beliefs and sharing with others.

More than half of all of the participants indicated a strong desire to express their personal values at work. These findings coincide with research that indicates that worker retention and loyalty correlate with shared values between employees and organizations.[20] When asked the reasons for the desire to express personal values at work, one third of the respondents stated that work is a large part of their lives and they want to be able to be themselves on the job. Nearly a third indicated that expressing their personal values at work would make them feel more peaceful on the job. One-in-four indicated that expressing their personal values at work would decrease the stress of the job.

Each of these findings correlates with research that suggests that workers desire to integrate their personal values into their work life for greater personal contentment.[21]

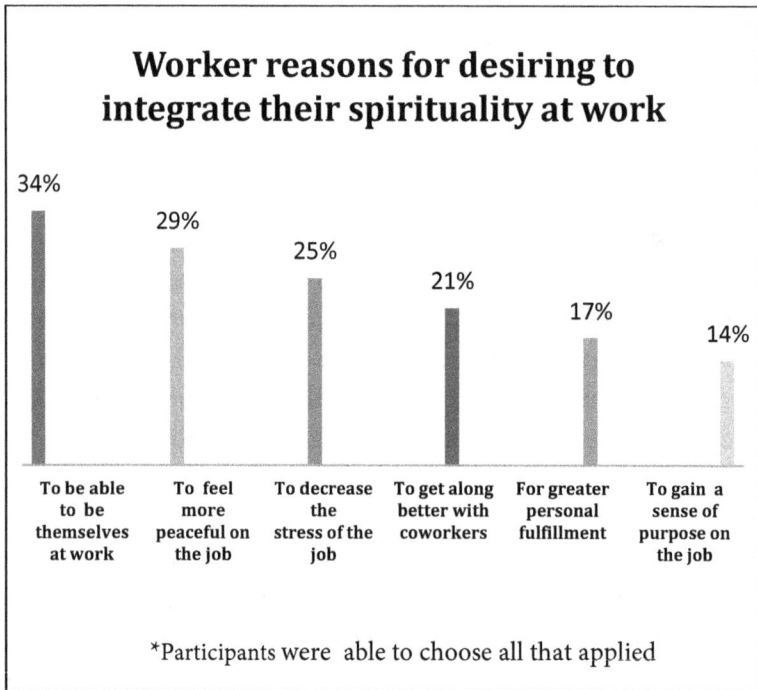

Worker reasons for desiring to integrate their spirituality at work

34%	29%	25%	21%	17%	14%
To be able to be themselves at work	To feel more peaceful on the job	To decrease the stress of the job	To get along better with coworkers	For greater personal fulfillment	To gain a sense of purpose on the job

*Participants were able to choose all that applied

When asked how they would feel about working in an environment where everyone is able to express their personal values, spirituality, or religious beliefs, six-in-ten of the participants responded agreeably. These findings are indicative of the participants' openness to allow others to express their spirituality in the workplace. In developing formal approaches to spirituality in the workplace, organizations will have to implement measures that allow for the respectful acceptance and expression of distinctive values and beliefs without encroachment on individual or groups' religious ideologies.

When asked to rank luxury and material goods with personal relationships and intangibles like meaning in life, relationship with God, environmental efficiency, faith, and family, over a third of the participants chose relationship with God as most important. Another third ranked family and personal relationships as most important, followed by faith.

Overall, my research indicates that the expression of spirituality in the workplace is tantamount to employees expressing their personal values which include the following:

- Demonstrating love for fellow human beings
- Developing friendships and other personal relationships at work
- Demonstrating love and obedience to God
- Respecting other people's values and beliefs
- Self-sacrifice
- Living in peace with others

My findings support additional research which highlights feelings of well-being and inner satisfaction among workers whose personal values and organizational values correspond.[22] Secondly, my findings affirm that the expression of spirituality in the workplace increases social capital. Additional research confirms that reciprocity and trust, which develop out of increased social capital, are enhanced in work environments where employees can express their spirituality.[23]

Coca-Cola Bottling Company and Ford Motor Company are among a growing number of organizations that allow and encourage employees from diverse religious and spiritual backgrounds to express their personal values at work. Ford allows the after hour's use of company facilities and the distribution of newsletters that engage workers in the expression of their spirituality. [24] Additionally, the company has created the Ford Interfaith Network, which has members representing Buddhism, Catholicism, Church of Jesus Christ of Latter-day Saints, evangelical Christianity, Hinduism, Islam, Judaism, and Orthodox Christianity. Ford prides itself on its company values, which include family, integrity, and personal industriousness. [25] Coca-Cola leads its values statement with, "Our values honor God." Coca-Cola believes that since publicizing its respect for spirituality in the workplace that employee satisfaction has increased and the company has benefited by increased loyalty and performance.[26]

In an ideal workforce, organizations would pursue the spiritual fulfillment of workers out of altruistic appreciation for workers' dedication and loyalty to their employers. That being said, in the absence of such benevolent considerations, business leaders and institutional heads must face the reality that spiritual hunger exists significantly among workers and that spiritual fulfillment affects worker satisfaction and worker satisfaction will undoubtedly affect organizational success. One reason for this is the effect of worker satisfaction on customer service.

Customers interact with employees as a first line of contact and the degree to which workers feel connected and validated is exhibited in their communications with clients. In cases where workers' interactions with customers is little or non-existent, company profits are still affected by worker satisfaction. Workers who are fulfilled are more likely to be dedicated and fully engaged in their work, whereas workers who are dissatisfied are more likely to be distracted, indifferent, absent, and less caring about quality.

Organizations that seek to recognize, understand, and meet the needs of workers will realize the benefits of increased worker performance and, ultimately, higher profits. What workers considered previously as an honest day's pay is no longer defined in mere dollars and cents. To a growing extent, workers are redefining work to include genuine fulfillment of their spiritual needs. Monetary exchange is only one component of remuneration that today's workers expect. The growing dissatisfaction among workers who believe that they are treated as mere physical beings on the job will likely begin to affect company success for two reasons.

Firstly, today's workers view the physical, emotional, and spiritual aspects of themselves as implicit, needful, and deserving of acknowledgment. Secondly, growing numbers of recruits are unwilling to deny these facets of their personhood at potential workplaces. Just as organizations assess potential employees for fit, prospective employees are evaluating companies to determine if they cultivate the kind of work environment that will yield the greatest level of inner satisfaction for workers.

Organizations traditionally link employee productivity to profits while emphasizing the benefits of physical output.[27] Perhaps this accounts for why employees have, over time, begun to describe their employers' growing expectations as spiritually burdensome. Followers resent being treated solely as physical beings with little or nothing to contribute creatively. While most workers may not disagree with the expectation of physical output, workers tend to disagree with having their emotional and spiritual needs go unmet in the process of performing at the job. Employees have become resistant to being defined as mere means to companies' ends. Spirituality has become a dominant and essential component of contemporary workers' collective identity.

Outspoken and assertive workers are demanding that organizations place less emphasis on quantifying physical work as the only way of measuring productivity and develop methods of self-appraisal that evaluate companies' efforts to cultivate the most productive environment for workers.

Contrary to organizational expectations, workers can psychologically withdraw from the job even if they remain there physically. When this happens employees may deliberately operate like the mere physical beings they believe they are treated as: without feelings or emotional or spiritual enhancement to their performance. Moreover, high turnover results from worker dissatisfaction. When dissatisfied employees resign, companies can spend between 1.75 and 3.5 times an employee's salary to recruit and train each replacement. Dissatisfaction among workers poses a threat and a serious problem for organizations, but not one without a solution.

Workers have provided the solution to companies by expressing their needs for a spiritually nurturing work environment. More and more people are searching for a work environment where they can express intrinsic needs, especially in light of the life invasive nature that has become characteristic of some job descriptions. As the tide of employee demands continues to rise in the area of spiritual fulfillment, it is likely that companies that demonstrate a measurable appreciation for employees' spiritual and emotional needs will begin to realize higher overall profits than companies whose focus is mainly on maintaining tradition.

Innovation is the major key to sustainability, especially in the global spectrum. Fulfilled employees are creative employees and creativity is what spurs ascendancy in any market. It follows then that it is in the best interest of organizations to invest in their survival, profitability, and competitiveness by investing in the human capital that is their employees. Because of the reciprocal nature of the worker-manager relationship, a worker who has emotional and spiritual needs fulfilled at work is likely to exhibit more loyalty, trust, and commitment to the organization and the quality of its goods and services than one who does not.

Therefore, in the interest of organizational sustainability, if nothing else, it is imperative that leaders begin to recognize the expediency of developing and cultivating organizational approaches to spirituality.

Spirituality and spiritual fulfillment are no small considerations for the new generation of workers. Spiritual expression that is not relegated to life outside of the workplace will likely yield an appreciative benefit, not just for the worker, but for the progressive organization.

THE DYNAMIC OF

POWER

"The Door is Open

and the Baby is Alive"

At the original penning of this work, African American research scholar and Harvard Professor, Dr. Henry Louis Gates, awaits a public apology from Sergeant James Crowley and the Cambridge, Massachusetts police department. Dr. Gates had been mistaken for a burglar by Lucia Whalen, a circulation and fundraising manager for Harvard Magazine, who, as a passerby, called the police stating that she observed two African American men attempting to enter someone's home around 12:45 in the afternoon. Upon receiving the 911 call, Sergeant Crowley responded to the home in question and, instead of encountering a pair of burglars, Sergeant Crowley met Dr. Gates who apparently had been struggling with a jammed lock at the front door of his own home.

Conflict arose during what became a heated discourse between the police officer and Dr. Gates, who ended up arrested and carted away in handcuffs despite displaying identification, proving his identity and ownership of the home he had entered. Dr. Gates was not charged with burglary, but with disorderly conduct for what may have amounted to talking back.

Opinions about Sergeant Crowley's handling of his encounter with Dr. Gates are plenteous and polarizing. It has been stated that people of color who have had experiences with police are unnerved though not surprised by the sergeant's actions against Dr. Gates as, for them, Sergeant Crowley's actions toward Dr. Gates are representative of the everyday experiences of Blacks in America, suggesting further that had it not been for Dr. Gates' status as a legendary historian and scholar, the incident would likely have gone unacknowledged by media or political pontificators. My father, an eighty-year old African American man whom I interviewed for this project commented, "Any Black man in America who is old enough to walk the streets alone is all too familiar with racial profiling."

In what appeared to be an effort to quell national unrest, President Barack Obama invited Sergeant Crowley and Dr. Gates to the Whitehouse. This, on the heels of President Obama's highly publicized critic of the police officers' as having behaved "stupidly," may have been an effort to redress any perceived offense by Cambridge Police. To the many vociferous objections to the President's gesture, my wise dad responded as follows.

Considering the issue around the President and his attempt to reconcile a situation that seems irreconcilable to the satisfaction of all interested parties, I address my personal opinion, however unpopular. Let us go back to King Solomon when he offered each mother one-half of the baby:

Some time later, two prostitutes came to the king to have an argument settled. "Please, my lord," one of them began, "this woman and I live in the same house. I gave birth to a baby while she was with me in the house. Three days later, she also had a baby.

We were alone; there were only two of us in the house. But her baby died during the night when she rolled over on it. Then she got up in the night and took my son from beside me while I was asleep. She laid her dead child in my arms and took mine to sleep beside her And in the morning when I tried to nurse my son, he was dead! But when I looked more closely in the morning light, I saw that it wasn't my son at all." Then the other woman interrupted, "It certainly was your son, and the living child is mine." "No," the first woman said, "the dead one is yours, and the living one is mine." And so they argued back and forth before the king.

Then the king said, "Let's get the facts straight. Both of you claim the living child is yours, and each says that the dead child belongs to the other. All right, bring me a sword." So a sword was brought to the king. Then he said, "Cut the living child in two and give half to each of these women!" Then the woman who really was the mother of the living child, and who loved him very much, cried out, "Oh no, my

95

lord! Give her the child – please do not kill him!" But the other woman said, "All right, he will be neither yours nor mine; divide him between us!" Then the king said, "Do not kill him, but give the baby to the woman who wants him to live, for she is his mother!" Word of the king's decision spread quickly throughout all Israel, and the people were awed as they realized the great wisdom God had given him to render decisions with justice (1 Kings 3:16-28 [NLT]).

Subsequently, wisdom prevailed. But suppose neither woman had spoken out and the baby was cut in half. Some people would have blamed woman number one. Some would have blamed woman number two. Still others would have blamed Solomon. In the end, with no solution achieved, the result would have been two mothers at odds, possibly for life, an unpopular king, and, last but not least, a dead baby.

Consequently, all doors to undo a terrible deed would have been closed forever. These two people, the police officer and the professor, like the two women in Solomon's court, may or may not reach a compromise, but the door is open and the baby is alive!

As demonstrated by President Obama, leadership, by its very nature, carries the weight of responsibility.

Imagine responsibility with a voice of its own. Imagine the voice of responsibility calling out through the streets of Everytown, USA and in the main auditorium of the United Nations pleading for deference from the loyalists for change. Imagine responsibility bellowing its voice through the halls of justice, every corporate corridor, through institutional passageways and religious parsonages eager for listening ears and hearing hearts to acknowledge her message in the midst of conflict, contention, indifference, and strife.

It appears that the President is attempting to heed the voice of responsibility as she calls for an audience with the President to mend already strained relations. Was the voice of responsibility audible during the fateful encounter between Sergeant Crowley and Dr. Gates? Certainly. Was responsibility present, ready, and willing to take control in the midst of confusion and strife? Without question. Were there leaders present who had demonstrated responsible behavior in the past? Undeniably so. Then what went wrong?

There are a whole host of theorizers pontificating about fear and caution and racial profiling and "uncooperative" (aka, uppity) behavior. Put simply, what went wrong then is what has gone wrong in countless situations throughout history and continues to go wrong today. What went wrong is that human nature emerged. Pride birthed offense and conflict ensued.

Humans, by nature, are flawed beings who are plagued with decisions between right thinking and wrong thinking, righteous behavior and unrighteous behavior, selfishness and unselfishness, provocative actions and irresponsible reactions all day, every day. What went wrong is that righteous indignation collided with effrontery. The natural instinct to rule and control collided with the intrinsic resistance to dominance, submission, and subjugation.

Sergeant Crowley, who allegedly has a background in teaching police officers about the inappropriateness of racial profiling, is now fielding controversy over this very subject as it relates to his encounter with Dr. Gates. Dr. Gates, a scholar in African American history, having now become intimately familiar with the experiences of so many of his subjects, is at the pivotal place of fielding public opinion while the world watches, opines, and polarizes itself in either camp. Supporters of Sergeant Crowley and those of Dr. Gates accuse the other of wrong actions, behaviors, thoughts, and motives.

While actions are the easiest to weigh, genuinely discerning others' hearts is not only not easy, but quite frankly, impossible and an futile exercise in self-indulgent arrogance to try for three reasons. For one, housed in the heart of each human being are all an individual's clandestine ambitions, hidden motives, unanswerable questions, irreconcilable conflicts, insecurities, expectations, resentments, and prideful absolutions ever so carefully concealed from the peering eyes of the world. The prophet, Jeremiah wrote, "The heart is deceitful above all things, and desperately wicked: who can know it?"[28] Secondly, people rarely know their own hearts well enough to judge themselves let alone others. Lastly, people view the world and others through the lens of their own heart-shaped worldview, so it is no wonder that no one can really know the heart of another.

Responsible leadership begins with the understanding and acceptance that everyone, without exception, carries the burden of being flawed by nature. Although it is no large feat to recognize the impediments of others, it is no small one and can be quite a sobering exercise to acknowledge one's own propensities toward ill intentions and behaviors. Power and authority are inherent aspects of leadership and without articulating position; the implied nature of control can lend itself, if unchecked by humility, grounding, and sound reasoning, to reach beyond the boundaries of common sense.

Ego is a problem. Ego is a serious problem, especially when underpinned with audacity and power. And while the egoist walks away satiated with winning, victims are left to stagger through the wreckage of torn personhood. Despotic behavior in leadership always leaves casualties in its wake. Principled leadership seeks to acknowledge, empower, and carefully guard the dignity of others.

Responsible leadership, in its authentic sense, *is* principled leadership that seeks to give love, to embody love, and to be love consistently and without respect of persons or concern for the cost to personal ego. Love seeks not her own, neither does love flaunt herself, behave unseemly or rejoice in wrong.[29] Love is not easily offended or provoked like pride. Put simply, love has no ego. Responsible leadership shuns egoism, superiority, and the arrogance that devalues others' time, efforts, aspirations, and basic human worth. Irresponsible leadership abuses power and considers authority a right to be exploited at any inclination and not a privilege merely bestowed by followers or providence.

LEADER NEEDS AND

THE ABUSE OF POWER

Wellington Feyer,* Senior IT Project Manager of Davis International,* agreed to resign his position amidst a flurry of accusations ranging from endangering the health and safety of employees to various forms of harassment. The accusations stemmed from a lawsuit alleging that Feyer violated the human rights of 35 of the company's 50 employees. The employees allege that they were subjected to continuous harassment by Feyer. The harassment, according to court documents, consisted of unwanted night and weekend home visits, incessant phone calls and text messages, persistent bullying, threats, name calling, offensive and objectionable language, and degrading treatment over the 3 year period of Feyer's term with the organization.

When asked for comment, Wellington Feyer's superior, CEO Jan Davis,* stated that she had enthusiastically hired the MIT graduate 3 years ago because of his superior background in research in groundbreaking technology, but had become increasingly concerned about Feyer's eighty-hour work weeks, intensifying agitation, and insatiable demand for recognition and commentary at every project juncture.

---

* The names of persons and business have been changed to fictitious names.

The determination of Wellington Feyer's guilt or innocence is the function and responsibility of the court to which his case has been assigned.

The purpose of sharing his experience, however, is to emphasize how the behaviors of which Mr. Feyer is accused often manifest as indicators of a leader's unmet needs. Wellington Feyer's subordinates asserted that Feyer exploited their leader/follower relationship by abusing his legitimate right to exercise power over them. I offer suggestions as to how leaders can recognize their basic human needs in order to avoid the misuse of power.

According to David McClelland, individuals' basic human needs are acquired over time, shaped by life experiences, and divided into three categories: achievement, affiliation, and power. [30] Achievement-oriented leaders seek challenges at work and are project driven. They are high achievers who seek challenges and prefer to work with other achievement driven individuals. Achievement-oriented leaders experience frustration with subordinates and peers who are less driven than they are. Additionally, leaders with a high need for achievement crave feedback on their accomplishments. In the absence of feedback, achievement-oriented leaders may experience disappointment.

The Need for Achievement

Wellington Feyer is apparently a high achiever. A science and technology graduate of Massachusetts Institute of Technology, Feyer brought his competitive work ethic to Davis International hoping to help the fledgling organization establish itself as a formidable contender for the Bay Area technology market. Feyer took pride in his goal-oriented work ethic and did not limit his contribution to the organization to typical working hours or time spent at the office. He had hoped his eighty-hour work week and rapid turnaround time for projects would demonstrate his dedication to expeditiousness and excellence. Feyer was proud of his achievements. Over the last several months, however, he had grown noticeably irritated with the lack of commitment he perceived in his peers and subordinates and the obvious indifference from his boss. Feyer determined that his subordinates required more oversight and his superior needed to pay closer attention to Feyer's efforts.

Although justifiably dedicated to company performance, Feyer's behavior demonstrates that he was, in reality, seeking to satisfy his unmet need for achievement. Typical of leaders with a high need for achievement, Feyer took on challenging projects and worked diligently to accomplish his goals. However, in so doing, Feyer obliged his subordinates to work with him at his pace without regard for their individual work capacities. Feyer admitted requiring his subordinates to work extra hours, including weekends, and saw nothing wrong with phoning about projects, sending text messages, and visiting his subordinates' homes for impromptu meetings on their days off.

Typical of individuals with a high need for achievement, Feyer became frustrated with the reality that he was working with people who were either less capable or less achievement motivated than he. Feyer had essentially sought to mold his subordinates into mirror images of himself so that his need to work with other high achievers would be met. While a certain degree of narcissistic behavior might characterize leaders generally,[31] the danger lies in attempting to mold subordinates into image of the leader. Wellington Feyer abused his power in his relationships with his followers by exerting undo pressure upon them to perform beyond their capacities.

The Need for Affiliation

Affiliation-oriented individuals need to be liked. They vigorously pursue harmonious relationships with others and will engage in most any level of compromise or acquiescence to gain camaraderie. Objective decision-making is usually difficult for affiliation-oriented leaders because they readily conform to group norms often compromising their own viewpoints. In general, individuals with a high need for affiliation tend to avoid leadership positions for fear of isolation.

Wellington Feyer's behaviors do not demonstrate that his need for affiliation was unmet. In fact, Feyer appeared not to be concerned about being liked; especially when he made the decision to push his subordinates to demonstrate their commitment to him and the organization at considerable expense to their individual identities and wellbeing. Feyer's behavior was the antithesis of a person with a high need for affiliation. Feyer was achievement oriented and not needy in the area of cultivating harmonious relationships. While Feyer was not necessarily motivated by a high need for affiliation, his relational capacities with followers were severely lacking and inhibited. Characteristic of a person with a high need for affiliation, Feyer demonstrated difficulty in objective decision-making; not because he conformed too readily to group norms, but because he was blinded by his quest to satisfy his unmet need for power.

The Need for Power

The need for power distinguishes itself into two sub-categories: (a) the need for institutional power and (b) the need for personal power.[32] Leaders who have a high need for institutional power focus their energies on galvanizing support for organizational goals and objectives. Leaders who have a high need for institutional power generally make more effective leaders than those with a high need for personal power because of their motivation to pursue a unified effort toward organizational success. Conversely, leaders with a high need for personal power seek primarily to control others' behaviors and though desirous of leadership positions, they can often lack the required affability and emotional intelligence to succeed.

Wellington Feyer's behaviors demonstrate a high need for personal power. Feyer's constant hovering over subordinates, blatant disregard for their individuality and his dictatorial style made him tyrannical and ineffective. Feyer's high need for personal power became apparent in his conduct with both subordinates and superiors. In forcing his subordinates to increase their work hours, Feyer sought to control how his subordinates spent the majority of their time. Feyer's incessant telephone calls, text messages and home visits also contributed to his insatiable need to establish a commanding presence in his followers' lives. Feyer calculatingly ensured that his subordinates' time and energies were consumed with anxieties relating to fulfilling his requests.

In addition to over-working them, Feyer further exploited his followers by regularly badgering and intimidating them through degrading treatment. The angst that Feyer cultivated in his subordinates resulted in a lowering of their resistance. This paved the way for him to increase the levels of disrespect and humiliation until his followers were completely overwhelmed, broken, and depleted. In essence, Feyer sought to amass power by neutralizing his followers' dignity and self-worth through a steady progression of antagonism, alienation, and fear.

Typical of an individual with a high need for personal power, Feyer also sought to fulfill his need through recognition. As expressed by Feyer's superior, Jan Davis, Feyer constantly demanded acknowledgement for his work. He craved regular feedback and recognition for his accomplishments despite the inability of his supervisor to compliment him daily. Essentially, Wellington Feyer abused his power in his relationships with his subordinates and superior through debasement and vexation.

While the needs for achievement, affiliation, and power are present in most people, there is usually a prevailing orientation that defines one's dominant motivation.[33] Wellington Feyer's unmet achievement and power needs fueled his propensity toward satisfying those needs and inevitably shaped his perceptions and behaviors in his relationships with others.

Although Wellington Feyer may be an atypical example of organizational leaders, aspects of his depiction are emblematic of how a leader's unmet needs can precipitate power abuse in relationships with followers. According to researcher, David Kipnis, power can have the following effects on leaders and followers.[34]

1. Power can influence leaders to increase their attempts to control the behavior of followers.

2. Power can in influence leaders to devalue followers' worth.

3. Power can in influence leaders to take undeserved credit for followers' performance.

4. Power can influence leaders to view followers as objects of manipulation.

5. Power can influence leaders to desire to distance themselves from followers.

As Wellington Feyer demonstrated, power abuse begins with volition. The decision, conscious or unconscious, to abuse power lead Wellington Feyer to the execution of the aforementioned power strategies designed to afflict followers and gratify his need to be in charge. According to French and Raven, there are five main sources of power.[35]

1. Power based on the ability to grant rewards

2. Power which is coercive and has the ability to Punish

3. Power that is legitimate which is based on position or authority

4. Referent power which identifies with whom or what the leader represents

5. Power which is grounded in knowledge or expertise

In the case of Wellington Feyer, coercive power was used to influence and control the behaviors of others. Misappropriated reward power, legitimate power, and referent power were also elements in Feyer's tactics to lord his authority and position over his subordinates.

It is quite possible that Wellington Feyer would deny his high need for personal power and defer instead to his strong work ethic and frustration with lazy subordinates. It is also plausible that Feyer would mildly acknowledge his degrading treatment of others as his need to slow down and not be so easily provoked by others' ineptitude. Like Feyer, leaders may not always perceive themselves as they present themselves to others. Therefore, it is imperative for leaders' personal integrity, character, respect for the positions they hold and the dignity of those they supervise to examine themselves honestly.

Leader Self Examination

Leaders' needs, motivations, and propensities and subordinates' dependencies inform the need for organizations to employ codes of conduct and systems of accountability that guard against the abuse of power. Leader credibility should be the complement to follower vulnerability and while leaders may resist transparency mechanisms, they are essential for maintaining employee confidence amidst power structures that by design sanction leaders' behaviors.

Secondly, and perhaps most importantly, leaders must learn to recognize their unmet needs and pursue ways of fulfilling those needs that avoid injurious behaviors toward others. The Thematic Apperception Test, developed by David McClelland, is a viable and respected instrument used by leaders to assess personality traits and inclinations.[36] Though developed more than a few years ago, the Thematic Apperception Test continues to prove relevant for contemporary leaders. Leaders who take the Thematic Apperception Test are likely to discover unconscious aspects of their personality that reveal hidden motives and needs for achievement, affiliation, and power.

By appraising one's needs through the Thematic Apperception Test or other reliable instrument a leader may be able to identify unmet needs. Once a leader establishes his unmet needs, the process can begin to examine the motives behind leadership career choices and the dominant personality traits that influence one's behavior. Leaders with a high need for institutional power are generally more successful as leaders than those with a high need for personal power because leaders with a high need for institutional power observably demonstrate more interest in building consensus and teambuilding, whereas leaders with high needs for personal power tend to exhibit myopic perceptions. They tend to be inwardly focused with a lack of flexibility and poor people skills.

Leaders with a high need for institutional power have been shown to be more effective than leaders with a high need for affiliation because leaders with a high need for affiliation tend to prioritize harmony in their relationships above objective decision-making. Leaders with a high need for institutional power may also be more effective than leaders with a high need for achievement because leaders with a high need for achievement tend to want to avoid conflict and can be risk averse.

Notwithstanding the possibilities that no dominant trait may yield all the necessary ingredients for exemplary leadership, and that savvy leaders learn to surround themselves with people who possess complementary strengths, leaders in every category have the responsibility to exercise power appropriately and with respect for the dignity of others. It is morally imperative that leaders begin to recognize their unmet needs and make every responsible effort to address their needs in ways that avoid the abuse of power in relationships with followers.

WHERE ORGANIZATIONS AND LEADERS GO FROM HERE:

THE SOCIAL-SPIRITUAL

Leaders have long defined organizational success by efficiency, advantage, and continual growth. Contemporary strategic planning suggests that fluidity enables organizations to adjust to environmental factors likely to affect performance. One such environmental factor I consider increasingly relevant is societal spirituality. Spiritual hunger, as exhibited by workers, points to major fulfillment longings within society as a whole and is, therefore, an environmental factor worthy of deliberate inclusion.

Societal spiritual hunger is not a recent phenomenon. From the onset of human existence individuals and groups have sought to fulfill inner longings of meaning and purpose through any number of outlets and expressions. Decades of psychological discourse point to the assertions of Abraham Maslow and the like for the almost inexplicable, though consistent, human pursuits leading ultimately to self- actualization.[37] Human psycho-social development somehow depends upon a cooperative awareness of individuals' needs for self-expression and integration. Inherent within the constructs of various societal groupings are value systems designed to reflect basic beliefs about everything from familial and other relationships to spirituality and the pursuits of significance and power.

The quest for spiritual fulfillment has been surfacing more and more conspicuously during the latter half of the twentieth century as familial relationships suffer unprecedented breakdowns and the imagined completeness anticipated by profligacy and the amassing of money, power, and position proves hollow. A nagging sense of futility haunts people young and old, strong and weak, poor and rich. Television psychics and others promising answers to life's most plaguing ponderings continue to grow in popularity. Social networking sites and mobile interfaces allow people to constantly engage each other. The plethora of television and online dating sites multiply to meet the demand for emotional, physical, and spiritual connection. Even most online gaming involves interaction between players at opposite ends of computers. As paradoxical as it seems, each of these technologically assisted mechanisms is in place to support the escalating demand for human-to-human engagement and affiliation.

At the root of desire for connection, meaning in life, and purpose is spiritual hunger. Organizations that would develop a responsive appreciation for societal spiritual hunger will have to commit, first of all, to employing value systems that reflect an understanding of the encompassing nature of human spirituality. Human spirituality is life defining. Particular processes by which 21st century organizational leaders may propose to explore and address the issue of societal spiritual hunger depend upon the extent to which organizations are willing to delve into moral codes heretofore eluded.

Marketing expenditures attest to corporations' awareness and efforts to acknowledge, at least superficially, societal spiritual hunger. Advertisements promising the intangibles of peace, acceptance, esteem, relationship, and prowess - intellectual and otherwise - to anyone and everyone utilizing particular products and services flood the media day and night. Whether truthful or deceptive, corporate advertising demonstrates a keen awareness that spiritual hunger exists and that the expectant outcome of corporate promise met by societal pursuit is indeed a viable contributor to the sway of market forces.

Social-spiritual consciousness carries with it, however, a certain self-governing ethical responsibility that compels considerations beyond economic advantage. Social-spiritual consciousness among leaders obliges organizations to take the notions of social responsibility beyond civic and legislative duties to the realms of demonstrated empathy and compassion. Though far-fetched, it is not inconceivable that corporations, through leaders, can begin to redirect ambitions away from the singular quest for economic imperialism to at least some appreciative support for humane working conditions, collaborative goal setting, and entrepreneurial fairness.

Multinational corporations and organizations in general are garnering progressively more power over workers, constituents, and consumers, especially in light of recent policy changes that open the floodgates of political influence to organizations. To that end, organizational leaders must begin to take stock of the very real responsibility that comes with unbridled power. Most organizations have power to exploit every advantage as well as power to exercise humanity and restraint. Corporations, though bound toward self-advancement by any legal means necessary, have, however, the freedom to participate in articulations that progress beyond the rhetoric of social consciousness to demonstrated acceptance of social-spiritual responsibility.

Social-spiritual responsibility entails, in short, doing right because it's right. Moral relativity falls short of providing a sufficient rationale for contributing to turbulence and instability around the world. Organizations and policy makers need to acknowledge and do away with entrenched values and belief systems that reduce individuals, groups, and communities to mere commodities to be exploited at every juncture. If corporations are indeed considered persons, then, as persons, corporations ought to be able to exercise the humaneness expected of any member of civil human society. Social-spiritual consciousness embraces the ethic of reciprocity and recognizes equity and fair play at home and in matters pertaining to global expansion. The power to marginalize or displace indigenous communities and businesses, for example, can indeed be left unexploited as a display of mere humanity. *"Do to others as you would like them do to you."*[38] The perpetuation of poverty and dependence among nations and people capable of contributing to global discourse and trade, and who simply need a hand up, as rationale for triple bottom line thinking only contributes to global antipathy and strife.

Social-spiritual responsibility resists organizational self-aggrandizement and reintroduces the concept of conscience by constraining power, communicating forthrightly, and demonstrating appreciation for the value and worth of human beings desirous of contributing to progress. With an eye toward the future of a volatile marketplace and the increasingly fragile state of human coexistence, political and organizational leaders must begin to engage in genuine and unfeigned discourse about the significance of individual spiritual fulfillment and its utter relation to human survival and peace.

Social-spiritual consciousness carries with it an imperative for change. Followers are no longer satisfied to acquiesce to the powers that be at the expense of individual expression of personhood. Reverend Jesse Jackson, in his May 12, 1968 address, recited his poem, "*I Am Somebody.*" His title phrase soon became a mantra among adults and children alike. Whether verbalized verbatim in the streets or not forty years later, this determination to assert self-worth continues to gain momentum with every political uprising, work stoppage, and riotous upheaval. Everybody wants to feel like somebody and the stakes for that realization are rising rapidly above the ability to contain escalating malcontent, and not just in the workplace.

Social-spiritual consciousness asserts that while a singular entity could theoretically consume an entire market, for example, in recognizing the spiritual needs of others it resists subjecting workers to feelings of marginalization and subjugation. Whether or not leaders intend to disenfranchise is immaterial. It is how leaders' actions are perceived that informs the condition of the leader/follower relationship. Leaders who understand the social-spiritual dynamic learn to acknowledge and appreciate the "somebody-ness" of everybody. Progressive, spiritually conscious leaders neither depend upon autocratic policies imposing yokes of conformity, nor do they lean on outdated assumptions of what followers accepted pre-twenty-first century, but rather embrace the understanding that purposeful and perceptible investment in human capital yield the returns of uncompelled performance and peace - that is, cooperative productivity resulting from meaningful and measurable contribution.

The value of peace cannot be overstated. Given the mushrooming state of unrest globally, organizational leaders must begin to reexamine priorities and redefine values. There is little enduring profit in gaining the whole world and losing the soul of an organization to rapacity and strife. Vexation of soul is at the heart of desperate attempts by followers and consumers to be heard, appreciated, and valued as human beings with lives and futures and families. The commodification of the marginalized and monetization of poor choices made by desperate people impede societal growth as a whole. At the heart of resisting the temptation toward indifference to workers' spiritual needs (which reflect larger society's) might well be love at its core. But if not for love, earnest contemplation of ultimate social and moral cost should suffice.

REFERENCES

Introduction: Leadership and Values

[1] Yukl, Gary. *Leadership in Organizations*. Fifth edition ed. Upper Saddle River: Prentice Hall, 2002.

[2] Ibid.

[3] "Number of Jobs Held, Labor Market Activity, and Earnings Growth Among the Youngest Baby Boomers: Results From a Longitudinal Survey Summary," *Bureau of Labor Statistics United States Department of Labor,* September 10, 2010, http://www.bls.gov/news.release/archives/nlsoy_09102010.pdf

The Dynamic of Communication

[4] *Holy Bible, Authorized King James Version.* Belgium: Thomas Nelson, 2001.

[5] *Holy Bible, People's Parallel Bible,* Carol Stream Tyndale House Publishers, Inc., 2005.

[6] Van Emmerik, I. J. Hetty. "The More You can Get the Better: Mentoring Constellations and Intrinsic Career Success." *Career Development International* 9, no. 6/7 (2004): 578.

[7] "Employee Discrimination in the Workplace." December 8 [cited 2009]. Available from http://media.gallup.com/government/PDF/Gallup_Discrimination_Report_Final.pdf

[8] Ibid.

[9] Hall, Edward T. *The Silent Language.* New York: Anchor Books, 1973.

[10] Bluedorn, Allen C. "An Interview with Anthropologist Edward T. Hall." *Journal of Management Inquiry* 7, no. 2 (Jun 1998): 109.

[11] Ibid.

[12] Hall, Edward T., and William Foote Whyte. "Intercultural Communication: A Guide to Men of Action." *The International Executive (Pre-1986)* 2, no. 4 (Fall 1960): 14.

[13] Chaisrakeo, Sunanta, and Mark Speece. "Culture, Intercultural Communication Competence, and Sales Negotiation: A Qualitative Research Approach." *The Journal of Business & Industrial Marketing* 19, no. 4/5 (2004): 267.

[14] Bluedorn, Allen C. "An Interview with Anthropologist Edward T. Hall." *Journal of Management Inquiry* 7, no. 2 (Jun 1998): 109.

[15] *United States Census 2000.* Washington: United States Census Bureau. 2000.

The Dynamic of Spirituality

[16] Putnam, Robert D. *Bowling alone: The collapse and revival of American community.* New York: Simon and Schuster, 2000.

[17] Worker Satisfaction Declines, Say Jobs are 'Just a Paycheck'. 2005. *IOMA's Report on Salary Surveys* 05, no. 4 (Apr) : 8.

[18] McBride, Lebron J. 2006. Effective Work Relationships: A Vital Ingredient in Your Practice. *Family practice management* 13, no. 10 (Nov/Dec): 45.

[19] Maharaj, Ishara, Anton F. Schlechter. 2007. Meaning in life and meaning of work: Relationships with organisational citizenship behaviour, commitment and job satisfaction. *Management Dynamics* 16, no. 3: 24.

[20] Milliman, John, Andrew J. Czaplewski, and Jeffery Ferguson. 2003. Workplace spirituality and employee work attitudes: An exploratory empirical assessment. *Journal of Organizational Change Management* 16, no. 4: 426.

[21] Ibid.

[22] Maharaj, Ishara, Anton F. Schlechter. 2007. Meaning in life and meaning of work: Relationships with organisational citizenship behaviour, commitment and job satisfaction. *Management Dynamics* 16, no. 3:

[23] Marques, Joan. 2008. Spirituality at Work: Internal Growth With Potential External Challenges. *The Journal for Quality and Participation* 31, no. 3 (Oct): 24.

[24] Grossman, Robert J. 2008. Religion at Work. *HR Magazine* 53, no. 12 (Dec): 26.

[25] Ibid.

[26] Ibid.

[27] Fairris, David. "Towards a Theory of Work Intensity." *Eastern Economic Journal* 30, no. 4 (Fall 2004): 587.

The Dynamic of Power

[28] *Holy Bible, Authorized King James Version*. Belgium: Thomas Nelson, 2001.

[29] Ibid.

[30] Harrell, Adrian M., and Michael J. Stahl. "A Behavioral Decision Theory Approach for Measuring McClelland's Trichotomy of Needs." *Journal of Applied Psychology* 66, no. 2 (Apr 1981): 242.

[31] Kets de Vries, Manfred. "A Clinical Look at Leaders." INSEAD Knowledgecast (November 2, 2006) Database on-line. Available from INSEAD, n6.

[32] McClelland, David. *Power: The Inner Experience*. 2nd Revised ed. New York: Irvington Publications, 1975.

[33] McClelland, David C. and Burnham, David H. *Power is the Great Motivator*. Boston: Harvard Business School Press, 2008.

[34] Kipmis, David. "Does Power Corrupt?" *Journal of Personality and Social Psychology* 24, no. 1 (20060329 1972): 33-41.

[35] Cuilla, Joanne B. ed., *Ethics, the Heart of Leadership*. 2nd ed. Westport, CT.: Praeger Publishers, 2004.

[36] Lundy, Allen. "The Reliability of the Thematic Apperception Test." *Journal of Personality Assessment* 49, no. 2 (April 1985): 141-145.

Conclusion: Where Organizations Go From Here: The Social-Spiritual

[37] Maslow, A. H. 1943. A Theory of Human Motivation. *Psychological Review* 50, no. 4 (July 19): 370-396.

[38] *Holy Bible, People's Parallel Bible*, Carol Stream Tyndale House Publishers, Inc., 2005.

www.ingramcontent.com/pod-product-compliance
Lightning Source LLC
Chambersburg PA
CBHW060046210326
41520CB00009B/1281